I0154221

Naval Academy United States

Regulations of the United States Naval Academy

As Approved by the Secretary of the Navy

Naval Academy United States

Regulations of the United States Naval Academy
As Approved by the Secretary of the Navy

ISBN/EAN: 9783744744102

Printed in Europe, USA, Canada, Australia, Japan

Cover: Foto ©ninafisch / pixelio.de

More available books at **www.hansebooks.com**

REGULATIONS

OF THE

UNITED STATES NAVAL ACADEMY

AS APPROVED BY THE

SECRETARY OF THE NAVY.

JANUARY 1, 1876.

WASHINGTON:
GOVERNMENT PRINTING OFFICE.
1876.

NAVY DEPARTMENT,
January 1, 1876.

The following regulations will be obeyed by all persons connected
with the Naval Academy.

GEO. M. ROBESON,
Secretary of the Navy.

CONTENTS.

PART I.—ACADEMIC ORGANIZATION.

Page.

I.—Government..
II.—Commandant of Cadets 9
III.—Senior Aid 10
IV.—Academic Board.. 10
V.—Heads of Departments 12
VI.—Instructors 13
VII —Senior Medical Officer 15
VIII.—Treasurer 15
IX.—Store-keeper.. 16
X.—Commissary 16
XI.—Secretary 17
XII.—Academic year 17
XIII.—Admission 18
XIV.—Classification 19
XV.—Course of instruction 19
XVL.—Examinations... 24
XVII.—Marks... 26
XVIII.—Merit-rolls.. 27
XIX.—Practice cruise.. 28
XX.—Register 29

PART II.—INTERIOR DISCIPLINE.

XXI.—Cadet organization 31
XXII.—Conduct... 32
XXIII.—Uniform of Cadets.. 35
XXIV.—Daily routine... 36
XXV.—Official intercourse....................................... 39
XXVI.—Religious services.. 40
XXVII.—Hospital... 41
XXVIII.—Library 42
XXIX.—Gymnasium 43
XXX.—Store.. 44
XXXI.—Grounds... 44
XXXII.—Cadets' quarters 45

6

	Page.
XXXIII.—Mess-hall	47
XXXIV.—Officer in Charge	48
XXXV.—Officer of the Day	50
XXXVI.—Superintendents of Floors and Buildings	53
XXXVII.—Superintendents of Rooms	54
XXXVIII.—Watchmen and Master-at-arms	54
XXXIX.—Formations	56
XL.—Section-leaders	56
XLI.—Section-rooms	57
XLII.—Reports and excuses	58
XLIII.—Leave of absence	59
XLIV.—Liberty	59
XLV.—Privileges	60
XLVI.—Fire organization	61
XLVII.—Barber's shop	61
XLVIII.—Bathing rooms	61
XLIX.—Boats	62
L.—Supplementary Regulations	62

PART I.—ACADEMIC ORGANIZATION.

I.—GOVERNMENT.

1. The United States Naval Academy shall be under the direct care and supervision of the Secretary of the Navy.

2. A line-officer of the Navy, of a rank not below that of Captain, shall be assigned by the Secretary of the Navy as Superintendent of the Naval Academy.

3. He shall be charged with the general superintendence and government of the Academy, and all Officers, Professors, Instructors and Cadets shall be under his command. He shall have charge of the grounds, buildings, vessels, and other public property, in use or belonging to the Academy. He shall have the power to appoint or remove all persons employed at the Academy, except those for whose employment or discharge special provision may be made by the laws, or regulations for the government of the Navy, or of the Academy.

4. At the end of each Academic month, he shall send a report of the marks and standing in each branch, and the number of demerits of each Cadet, to his parent or guardian; and a report of the relative standing of the Cadets in the various branches, and the number of demerits, to the Secretary of the Navy.

5. At the end of the first term, he shall transmit to the Secretary of the Navy the reports of the relative standing and demerits for the term, and the report of deficiencies, with the recommendations of the Academic Board, and he shall give a warning to Cadets whose averages in any uncompleted branch falls below 2.50, stating that their progress is unsatisfactory.

6. At the end of each Academic year, he shall cause the merit-roll of each class, for the year, to be made out, and the merit-roll of the graduating class for the course. He shall transmit to the Secretary of the Navy a copy of the graduating merit-roll, the reports of the relative standing of the Cadets in the three lower classes; and a report of deficiencies, similar to that sent at the end of the first term.

7. At the end of each term, he shall send a report of the marks and standing in each completed branch, and the number of demerits of each Cadet, to his parent or guardian, with a statement as to the final disposition of his case, if found deficient in any branch.

8. Officers of the Navy, on the application of the Superintendent, will be assigned to duty at the Academy by the Secretary of the Navy, as far as may be necessary to complete its organization.

9. All persons employed at the Academy shall be subject to these regulations.

10. No person connected with the Academy shall, unless authorized by the Secretary of the Navy, give any certificate, sign any paper, or take any action whatever, in relation to a decision of the Secretary of the Navy, or of the Academic Board, concerning any person who is, or who may have been, connected with the Academy, and no person connected with the Academy shall make any statement relative to the qualifications, standing, or character of any Cadet, or of any person who may have been a Cadet, or concerning the examination of any candidate for admission, unless authorized by the Secretary of the Navy, or by the Superintendent.

11. No person connected with the Academy shall cause publications, or correspond with official persons, in regard to transactions at the Academy, in a manner not authorized by the regulations for the government of the Navy.

12. No person connected with the Academy shall take or receive any present, or gratuity, directly or indirectly, from Cadets, or candidates for admission, or from their relatives or friends, without the approval of the Superintendent, nor shall any such person receive any compensation for tuition of Cadets, or candidates, or persons wishing to become candidates.

13. It shall be the duty of all officers, naval and civil, at the Academy, who have knowledge of any violation of a regulation, or of any neglect, or improper conduct of which a Cadet has been guilty, to report the fact to the Commandant of Cadets. Cases of negligence or impropriety on the part of any other person connected with the Academy may be reported by the person observing them to the proper officer.

14. Leave of absence may be granted by the Superintendent to any officers, naval and civil, attached to the Academy, from the close of one Academic year to the beginning of the next, provided that their services are not required, and at other times for shorter periods, at his discretion.

15. All officers, naval and civil, shall report their return from leave of absence to the officers from and through whom the leave was obtained.

16. No officer of the Navy shall exercise authority at the Academy, unless subordinate to the Superintendent.

II.—COMMANDANT OF CADETS.

17. The Commandant of Cadets shall be a line officer of the Navy, of a rank not below that of Commander, and he shall be next in command and authority to the Superintendent.

18. He shall have charge and supervision, under the orders of the Superintendent, of the police and police force of the Academy, including watchmen and marines, and of the fire department; and he shall perform such other duties as the Superintendent may direct, for the preservation of discipline, and for the general security.

19. He shall have general direction, subject to the control of the Superintendent, of all drills and tactical instruction in the departments of seamanship and gunnery.

20. He shall frequently, with the aid of his assistants, inspect the buildings used by the Cadets, and when any slight repairs are needed he shall send notice to the Senior Aid, to have the damage made good; but whenever alterations or expensive repairs shall be necessary he shall report the fact to the Superintendent. He shall call the attention of the Superintendent to whatever he may see amiss, or to any change that would conduce to the comfort or enjoyment of the cadets.

21. He shall, as second in command, report to the Superintendent any violation of the regulations that shall come to his knowledge on the part of any one attached to the Academy, or temporarily within its precincts, and he shall promptly and authoritatively check any such irregularity, using (if need be) the police force under his command for this purpose.

22. He shall submit the daily conduct report to the Superintendent, and shall cause it to be entered on the record as approved. No person except himself or his assistants shall have access to the record, nor shall its contents be communicated to any one, except for authorized public purposes, without a written order from the Superintendent.

23. At the end of each Academic month, term, and year, he shall report the number of demerits of each Cadet to the Superintendent, and he shall send a copy of the annual report of demerits to the officer charged with the prepararation of the merit-roll.

24. Whenever a Cadet is absent from a recitation without proper authority, the Commandant of Cadets shall notify the Head of the Department in which the recitation took place.

25. In the absence of the Commandant of Cadets his senior assistant shall perform the duties of his office.

III.—SENIOR AID.

26. The Senior Aid shall be a line officer of the Navy. He shall have charge, under the direction of the Superintendent, of the public lands and the buildings thereon; of the materials for the erection of buildings, and for repairs and improvements; and of all other property for which no other person is responsible. He shall, also, under the direction of the Superintendent, make purchases for the Academy, and shall have prepared the accounts, returns, and rolls relative to the public property under his charge, and to disbursements made by the Superintendent; and he shall, unless otherwise directed by the Superintendent, have control of the workmen employed in the erection or repairs of the public buildings, and in the improvement of the grounds.

27. Applications for repairs of quarters shall be made, in writing, to the Superintendent, through and under cover to his Senior Aid.

IV.—ACADEMIC BOARD.

28. The Academic Board shall be composed of the Superintendent, the Commandant of Cadets, and the Heads of Departments.

29. The Superintendent, or, in his absence, the Commandant of Cadets, shall preside at the meetings. In the absence of both, the senior officer present shall preside; but all reports and returns of the Board shall be made to or through the Superintendent.

30. Meetings shall be held on the last Monday of each Academic month, unless otherwise directed by the Superintendent, and at such other times as he may appoint; and a majority of the members shall constitute a quorum.

31. It shall be the duty of the Academic Board to prescribe, subject to the approval of the Secretary of the Navy, the subjects and arrangement of the course of instruction, and the text-books to be used; to regulate the recurrence of examinations; to determine the relative weight of marks for recitations and examinations in any department, on the recommendation of the Head of the Department; to fix the relative weight of the marks in different branches of study; to submit regulations, prepared in accordance with law, governing the examination for admission, which regulations shall be ready for publication by November 1 of each year; to make semi-annual and annual reports of the relative standing of Cadets, and of the marks, aptitude, habits, and conduct of Cadets found deficient, with recommendations as to the disposal of the latter; and "Cadets found deficient shall not be continued at the Academy or in the service, unless upon the recommendation of the Academic Board." (Revised Statutes, §§ 1519-1525.)

32. The rules of parliamentary proceedings shall govern at meetings of the Board; and in voting by ballot, the Superintendent shall have three votes, the other members one each.

33. The adjournment of the Board shall be directed by the presiding officer.

34. The Superintendent shall designate a suitable person, already attached to the Academy, as Secretary of the Board.

35. The deliberations of the Board shall be confidential, and no decision shall be disclosed by any person connected with the Board before the same shall be announced by proper authority.

36. A member, or members, of the Academic Board, assisted by such other officers as the Superintendent may direct, shall be detailed at the beginning of each year to prepare the tabular assignment of section-rooms, the Academic Calendar, the Annual Register, and the circulars issued to candidates for admission.

37. A committee of members of the Academic Board, designated by the Superintendent, at the regular meeting in December, shall conduct the examination of candidates for admission; and the same or another committee shall prepare the programmes for semi-annual and annual examinations; and the semi-annual and annual deficiency reports, the latter containing the names of all Cadets whose average in any branch for the term or year falls below 2.50, their final average in all branches, and the number of demerits: a statement of their aptitude and habits of study, aptitude for the service, and general conduct; and recommendations as to the disposal of each case. The reports, as modified or adopted by the Board, shall be forwarded by the Superintendent to the Secretary of the Navy.

38. A member of the Academic Board, assisted by such other officers as the Superintendent may direct, shall be charged with the preparation of the merit-rolls.

V.—HEADS OF DEPARTMENTS.

39. Heads of Departments shall have general charge and supervision of the instruction of Cadets in their respective departments.

40. The Head of each Department shall distribute the work of his department among the instructors assigned to duty as his assistants, and shall give such personal instruction in recitations, or lectures, as he may think proper. He shall arrange the classes under instruction in his department in sections, for purposes of recitation, and shall send the section-arrangement to the Commandant of Cadets for publication, as often as a change is made. He shall visit frequently the section-rooms of his assistants, and make such regulations as to the method of instruction and routine of recitations as may be necessary.

41. He shall keep a record of the books, instruments, apparatus, and other articles supplied to his department, and shall be responsible for all such articles.

42. He shall make duplicate weekly reports to the Superintendent, by 11.30 a. m. on Saturday, containing the names and averages of Cadets, in each branch of his department, whose average for the week falls below 2.5. One copy of each report shall be sent to the Superintendent, the other to the Commandant of Cadets for publication.

43. At the end of each Academic month he shall send to the Superintendent class-reports in each branch of study in his department, containing the names of Cadets arranged in the order of merit, with the class-numbers, weekly and monthly averages, examination-marks, and final averages. When semi-monthly examinations are held, a separate report of the marks of the first examination shall be sent to the Superintendent.

44. Before the first day of the last month of each term he shall send a report to the Superintendent of the examinations to be held at the end of the term in his department, the time required for each examination, the character of the examination, (whether written or oral,) and the formula for combining examination-marks with term-averages.

45. As soon as possible after the semi-annual and annual examinations he shall send to the Superintendent class-reports in each branch of study in his department, containing the names of Cadets in the order of merit for the term or year, with the class-numbers and the monthly, term, examination and final averages.

46. At the end of each Academic year he shall send, to the officer charged with the preparation of the merit-rolls, class-reports, in each branch taught in his department for which a co-efficient is allowed, containing the names of Cadets in the order of merit, with their class-numbers, final averages, and multiples.

47. Immediately after the close of the annual examination he shall send to the Secretary of the Academy in a sealed envelope, marked "Examination-papers, Department of ——," a copy of the examination-papers set at the semi-annual and annual examinations in his department, and a copy of specimen questions given at each oral examination. These papers shall be written without abbreviations, and on one side of the paper only.

48. He shall also, at the close of each Academic year, make requisition for such stationery, books, instruments, and apparatus as may be needed during the following year in his department, and shall inform the store-keeper as to the probable number of text-books and other articles that will be required by Cadets in the studies under his charge. He shall at the same time send to the Librarian a list of desirable books not in the library relating to the subjects of his department.

49. Heads of Departments in which monthly examinations are held shall meet on the first Monday of each Academic month, at the call of their senior officer, to prepare for publication a programme of examinations, and to designate examination-rooms for the month.

50. There shall be a Commander or Lieutenant Commander at the head of the department of Seamanship and of the department of Ordnance and Gunnery, who, with the other officers assigned to their departments, shall be the assistants to the Commandant of Cadets in carrying out the discipline of the Academy.

VI.—INSTRUCTORS.

51. Instructors shall carry on the work of instruction, examination, and attendance in section-rooms, under the orders of the

Head of the Department to which they are attached. They shall be ready to assist the Head of the Department in the performance of any duty which may fall to him by regulation or special order.

52. Instructors shall note the marks of Cadets in their section-books, and make weekly reports to the Head of the Department.

53. They shall have charge of the different sections in rotation according to the detail made out by the Head of the Department.

54. They shall be in their section-rooms at the sound of the bugle, and shall be responsible for the orderly conduct of sections in their charge; and they shall exact of Cadets, and especially of section-leaders, the strictest observance of the regulations in regard to bearing and general demeanor in section-rooms. Particular attention shall be paid to the manner in which sections enter and leave the room, to the formalities of rising and taking seats, and to the attitude of Cadets, seated or standing.

55. All reports of delinquencies occurring in recitations, lectures, or examinations in any department, except in cases of absence, shall be made through the Head of the Department.

56. Instructors shall dismiss their sections punctually at the first note of the recall, (except as specified in Article 57,) without regard to the progress of the recitation. All necessary directions as to the next lesson, or what not, shall be given at the beginning of the recitation.

57. In the case of sections reciting in the first hour of a period, the recitation may be prolonged fifteen minutes after the recall, if the section-room is vacant during the second hour, but in no other case, and in no case beyond this time.

58. Instructors ordered by the Superintendent or Commandant of Cadets, to any duty other than that connected with their department, or to routine duty as Officer in Charge, shall notify the Head of the Department without delay.

59. Officers detailed to assist the Commandant of Cadets in performing the duties of Officer in Charge, during the day or night, shall make application to him for leave of absence, before preferring their application to the Superintendent. Instructors will always first apply to the Head of the Department.

60. No Instructor shall have any communication with a Cadet on the subject of his marks unless the latter has received special permission from the Superintendent.

VII.—SENIOR MEDICAL OFFICER.

61. The Senior Medical Officer is directly responsible to the Superintendent for the care of the sick, the suggestion of measures for the maintenance of a proper hygiene, and the preservation and expenditure of public property belonging to his department.

62. He shall report daily to the Superintendent the names of all persons attached to the Academy who may be unfitted for duty by illness, and shall furnish to the Commandant of Cadets a daily sick-list and excused-list of Cadets.

63. He shall report to the Superintendent the name of any person feigning illness or disability, that he may be recommended to the Secretary of the Navy for dismissal.

64. If, in the opinion of the Senior Medical Officer, a Cadet is disqualified for the service, by any physical or mental cause, he shall report the fact to the Superintendent, who shall forward the report to the Secretary of the Navy, that he may submit the case, if he think proper, to a Medical Board, to determine whether or not the Cadet shall be retained in the service.

65. The Senior Medical Officer shall have immediate charge of all the subordinates in his department, and of all the sick, whether in hospital or quarters; and he shall, with the approval of the Superintendent, establish regulations for the hospital and dispensary, to which all invalids and Cadets shall conform.

66. All the Medical Officers of the Academy shall not be absent from the Academic limits at the same time, without special authority from the Superintendent.

VIII.—TREASURER.

67. An officer of the Pay Corps of the Navy shall be assigned to duty as Treasurer of the Academy.

68. The bills of the Store-keeper, Commissary, laundress, and barber, and the postage-account of each Cadet, certified by him, and approved by the Superintendent, shall be paid by the Treasurer, at the end of the month, and charged to the account of the Cadet.

69. The Superintendent may from time to time authorize the Treasurer to pay to the Cadets, or for them, such small sums of money as he may think proper.

70. Sixty dollars per annum of each Cadet's pay shall be reserved for the purchase of his outfit at graduation.

71. The Treasurer shall make to the Superintendent a monthly statement of the account of each Cadet, showing the amount paid and the balance due.

72. The accounts of the mechanics and laborers, signed by them respectively, and approved by the Superintendent, shall be made up and paid monthly by the Treasurer.

73. Bills for supplies furnished to the Academy, by order of the Superintendent and approved by him, shall be paid by the Treasurer.

IX.—STORE-KEEPER.

74. The Store-keeper of the Academy shall be detailed from the Pay Corps of the Navy, and he shall have the authority, with the approval of the Secretary of the Navy, to procure clothing and other necessaries for the Cadets, to be issued under such regulations as the Superintendent may prescribe.

75. The Store-keeper shall be furnished with a store-room within the Academic limits, in which he shall keep only such articles as may be authorized by the Superintendent.

76. He shall issue no article to Cadets without the written authority of the Superintendent or Commandant of Cadets.

77. He shall be at the store on Saturday by noon, and at such other times as may be necessary, or as the Superintendent may direct, or the Commandant of Cadets may require.

78. The account of each Cadet shall be submitted to the Superintendent on the last day of the month, and approved before being sent to the Treasurer.

79. A board of three officers shall be appointed by the Superintendent, who shall examine all articles provided by the Store-keeper, for the use of the Cadets, and shall compare the clothing to be issued with approved patterns. The board shall reject all such articles as, in its judgment, are not of suitable quality or price, or do not conform to prescribed orders or regulations.

80. The board shall, from time to time, make to the Superintendent such suggestions in regard to the Store-keeper's department as it may think proper.

X.—COMMISSARY.

81. A Commissary, appointed by the Superintendent, shall furnish the Cadets with only such articles of diet as the Superintendent may direct.

X.—THE COMMISSARIAT.

81. The duties pertaining to the Cadets' Mess-Hall shall be discharged by a Paymaster detailed as Commissary of the Naval Academy by the Navy Department; and by the Officer who, as Assistant to the Commandant of Cadets, is charged by the Superintendent with the discipline and police of the Mess-Hall.

82. The Paymaster-Commissary of the Naval Academy shall under instructions from the Superintendent, fix the dietary of the Mess-Hall; he shall be charged with the purchase and care, until issued for use, of all articles of provision, table-ware, table-linen, kitchen-ware, and stores in general, needed for the complete ordering of the Cadets' table and laundry; and he shall be responsible for the proper preparation and cooking of all articles of table consumption.

83. He shall, with the approval of the Commandant of Cadets, employ the cooks, and servants in general, who are required for the Mess-Hall and Kitchen.

84. He shall keep a set of books which shall at all times be open to a Board of Audit, appointed by the Superintendent, to inspect and pass upon his monthly accounts, prior to their submission to the Superintendent for his approval. The books shall show the monthly cost of maintaining the table and laundry for the Cadets, and the amounts to be charged therefor by the Treasurer against their individual accounts.

82. He shall present his accounts every month to a board of three officers, appointed by the Superintendent, to be audited; and, after approval by the Superintendent, the accounts shall be settled by the Treasurer.

83. He shall receive for his profits an amount not exceeding six per cent. per annum on expenditures for articles of food; and as a guarantee that the articles procured have been purchased at the lowest cash-price, he shall produce every bill, and certify that the articles have been received at the lowest market-rates; that no deductions other than those which appear upon the bills have been made, and that he receives no other profit, directly or indirectly, than the six per cent hereby authorized.

84. He shall keep a set of books, of creditor and debtor, in which he shall enter all articles purchased and expended; he shall keep on file all original bills receipted, and both bills and books shall be subject at all times to the inspection of the board of audit, or of the Board of Visitors.

XI.—SECRETARY.

85. The Secretary shall be appointed on the nomination of the Superintendent, with the approval of the Secretary of the Navy.

86. He shall conduct the correspondence of the Academy and keep the official records, as follows : Rolls of the Academy, which shall contain a list of the Cadets, with the name in full, date of admission, place of birth, age, place from which appointed, residence, name, and occupation of parents or guardians; monthly class-reports, conduct-rolls, merit-rolls, inventories of public property, and records of requisitions.

87. He shall make out the conduct and merit reports for the Navy Department, and file and preserve the public correspondence and other papers of the Academy.

88. He shall inform the Heads of Departments of all resignations, dismissals, and re-instatements.

XII.—ACADEMIC YEAR.

89. The Academic year shall begin September 20, and end June 20, consisting of two terms; the first term, from September 20 to the Saturday nearest to January 30; and the second term, from the close of the first term to June 20.

2

90. Each term shall contain four Academic months; those in the first term being named October, November, December, and January; and in the second, February, March, April, and May. The first Academic month of each term shall comprise the five weeks beginning with the first Monday of the term; and the two months following shall each comprise four weeks. The fourth month of the first term shall end on the Saturday nearest to January 23; and the fourth month of the second term on the Saturday nearest to June 4.

91. Studies and exercises shall be suspended on January 1, February 22, July 4, Thanksgiving Day, and Christmas Day, and after supper on Christmas eve.

XIII.—ADMISSION.

92. There shall be two examinations of candidates for admission as Cadet-Midshipmen, and one examination for admission as Cadet-Engineers, the dates of which shall be specified in the circulars published yearly for the information of candidates; no candidates will be examined at other times than those specified.

93. The examination for admission as Cadet-Engineers shall be competitive.

94. No candidate for admission as Cadet-Midshipman shall be examined if his age exceed 18 years, or be less than 14 years. (Revised Statutes, § 1577.)

95. No candidate for admission as a Cadet-Engineer shall be examined if his age exceed 20 years, or be less than 16 years.

96. All candidates will be required to certify on honor their exact age.

97. Circulars containing directions for candidates shall be prepared yearly by a committee of the Academic Board designated by the Superintendent.

98. The physical examination shall be conducted by a board of Medical Officers of the Navy convened for the purpose; and the mental examination by a committee of members of the Academic Board designated by the Superintendent; and no candidate shall be admitted unless, in the opinion of the two boards, he shows the requisite mental and physical qualifications.

99. Candidates rejected at the mental examination for admission as Cadet-Midshipmen "shall not have the privilege of another examination for admission to the same class, unless recommended by the Board of Examiners." (Revised Statutes, § 1515.)

100. Candidates who enter the Academy shall be allowed their actual and necessary traveling expenses from their residence to the Academy. But no allowance shall be made for board, or other expenses incurred, while in attendance at the examination, and any Cadet who voluntarily resigns his appointment within a year after the date of his admission will be required to refund the amount paid him for traveling expenses.

101. On becoming an inmate of the Academy, each Cadet shall take the prescribed oath, engaging himself to serve in the Navy of the United States for eight years, including the period of his probation as a Cadet, unless sooner discharged. He shall deposit with the Treasurer the sum of fifty dollars, for which he shall be credited on the books of that office; and this sum may be expended by the Superintendent in the purchase of text-books and other authorized articles for his use. In addition to this sum, he shall make a deposit for clothing and furniture, the amount of which shall be specified in the annual circular. Both deposits shall be made before the candidate is received into the Academy.

XIV.—CLASSIFICATION.

102. The Cadet-Midshipmen shall be arranged in four classes, and the Cadet-Engineers in four classes, corresponding to the four years of instruction.

103. Cadets pursuing the first year's course shall form the fourth class; the second year's course, the third class; the third year's course, the second class; and the fourth year's course, the first class.

104. The Cadet-Midshipmen and Cadet-Engineers may be arranged together in sections, when pursuing the same studies; but weekly reports of unsatisfactory recitations, and reports of class-standing for the month, term, and year shall be made out for Cadet-Midshipmen and Cadet-Engineers separately.

COURSE OF INSTRUCTION.

105. The branches of study taught at the Academy shall be grouped under the following departments:
1. Seamanship.
2. Ordnance and Gunnery.
3. Mathematics.

4. Steam-Engineering.
5. Astronomy and Navigation.
6. Physics and Chemistry.
7. English Studies, History, and Law.
8. Modern Languages.
9. Drawing.

106. The course of study shall embrace the following subjects:

Department of Seamanship.

Seamanship.—The material and manufacture of all kinds of rope; knotting and splicing; the masting, sparring, and rigging of ships; stowage; the organization of a ship's company; the management and equipment of boats; handling sails; the management and evolutions of vessels; the duties of officers; the laws of storms, and the rules of the road.

Ship-building.—The construction of ships and docks, and the launching and docking of vessels.

Naval Architecture.—The designing of ships, including the necessary calculations.

Naval Tactics.—The organization and manœuvring of fleets.

Practical Exercises.—In Seamanship, with sails and spars; in Naval Tactics, with boats, and in signals. The instruction in boxing, swimming, gymnastics, and dancing shall be in charge of this department.

Department of Ordnance and Gunnery.

Ordnance and Gunnery.—Metallurgy in its relation to gun-metals; the manufacture of guns, gunpowder, and projectiles; pyrotechny; trajectories; field-fortifications.

Ordnance Instructions.—The Ordnance Instructions issued by the Bureau of Ordnance.

Infantry Tactics.—The school of the soldier, company, and battalion.

Practical Exercises.—Infantry-drill; field-artillery and boat-howitzer exercise; exercise and target-practice with great guns; mortar-practice and fencing.

Department of Mathematics.

Algebra.—Fundamental operations; reduction and conversion of fractional and surd quantities; involution and evolution; reduction and solution of equations of the first and second degrees; the summation of series; the nature, construction, and use of logarithms; the theory of equations.

Geometry.—Plane and solid geometry, the mensuration of surfaces and volumes; the application of algebra to geometry.

Trigonometry.—Analytical investigation of trigonometric formulas, and their application to all the cases of plane and spherical trigonometry; the construction and use of trigonometric tables; the solution of trigonometric equations; trigonometric series.

Analytical Geometry.—Equations of the right line, plane, and conic sections; discussion of the general equation of the second degree involving two or three variables; determination of loci; principal problems relating to the cylinder, cone, sphere, and spheroid.

Descriptive Geometry.—The graphic illustration and solution of problems in solid geometry, and the application of the method, particularly to the projections of the sphere, and the construction of maps.

Department of Steam-Engineering.

Marine Engines.—General theory of the steam-engine; classification and details of marine steam-engines, and of instruments and apparatus used in connection with them; the principles followed to insure strength in construction; the computation of the power and its cost; the duties of the engine-room watch, and of the engineer division.

Fabrication of Machinery.—The qualities and strength of materials, and the processes of manufacture.

Designing of Machinery.—The designing and construction of engines and other machinery, and the motions employed in valve-gearing.

Mechanical Drawing.—The nomenclature of design and construction; general and conventional practices of the art; the execution of plans, elevations, and sections.

Practical Exercises.—The management of marine steam-apparatus; the use of tools and machines; hand-work of the machine-shop, pattern-shop, smithery, boiler-shop, and foundery.

Department of Astronomy and Navigation.

Astronomy.—Descriptive and practical astronomy, including the use of instruments, especially those used in determining terrestrial latitude and longitude.

Navigation.—Theoretical and practical navigation, including instruction in the duties of the navigator, the use of navigating-instruments and their construction, with the solution of problems and the use of tables.

Surveying.—Geodetical and nautical surveying; practical work in surveying and constructing charts.

Department of Physics and Chemistry.

Chemistry.—General chemistry; chemistry of explosives; qualitative analysis.

Physics.—Acoustics, optics, heat, electricity, and magnetism.

Applied Mathematics and Mechanics.—The differential calculus; applications to problems of maxima and minima, and to the theory of curves. The integral calculus; definite integrals; differential equations. Statics. Dynamics, including the motion of bodies; rotation about an axis; central forces; the laws of planetary motion, and the motion of projectiles. Hydrostatics and hydrodynamics.

Experimental lectures in Physics and Chemistry.

Department of English Studies, History, and Law.

Law.—Constitution of the United States; International Law.

History.—History of English Colonies in North America, and of the United States. Outline of European history. Naval history of the United States.

Rhetoric, and exercises in English composition, consisting of themes and official reports.

English.—History, usage, and grammatical structure of the English language.

Department of Modern Languages.

The grammar of the French and Spanish languages, and exercises in reading, writing, and conversation.

Department of Drawing.

Line-drawing, topography, and free-hand drawing.

107. The course of instruction shall extend over four years, and the course of each year shall be as follows :

FIRST YEAR.

Cadet-Midshipmen.

Algebra, Geometry, English History, French, Drawing. Practical instruction in Seamanship, Naval Tactics, Great Guns, Infantry Tactics, Field-Artillery, Boat-Howitzers, Fencing, Dancing, Swimming.

Cadet-Engineers.

Algebra, Geometry, English, French, Mechanical Drawing. Practical instruction in use of tools, Marine Engines, Great Guns, Infantry Tactics, Field-Artillery, Fencing, Dancing, Swimming.

SECOND YEAR.

Trigonometry, Descriptive Geometry, Analytical Geometry, History, Rhetoric, Elementary Physics, Chemistry, French, Drawing (free-hand.) Practical instruction in Seamanship, Naval Tactics, Great Guns, Infantry Tactics, Field-Artillery, Boat-Howitzers, Signals, Fencing, Gymnastics.

Trigonometry, Descriptive Geometry, Analytical Geometry, History, Rhetoric, Elementary Physics, Chemistry, French, Mechanical Drawing. Practical instruction in the use of tools, Marine Engines, Great Guns, Infantry Tactics, Field-Artillery, Signals, Fencing, Gymnastics.

THIRD YEAR.

Seamanship, Ship-building, Naval Tactics, Infantry Tactics, Ordnance Instructions, Astronomy, Applied Mathematics, Mechanics, Electricity, French, Spanish, English Composition. Practical instruction in Seamanship, Naval Tactics, Great Guns, Infantry Tactics, Field-Artillery, Boat-Howitzers, Signals, Fencing, Boxing.

Ship-building, Fabrication and Designing of Machinery, Marine Engines, Mechanical Drawing, Applied Mathematics, Mechanics, Electricity, French, Spanish, English Composition. Practical instruction in the use of tools, Marine Engines, Great Guns, Infantry Tactics, Field-Artillery, Signals, Fencing, and Boxing.

Seamanship, Naval Architecture, Ordnance and Armor, Navigation and Surveying, Marine Engines, Light, Heat, Spanish, Public Law. Practical instruction in Seamanship, Naval Tactics, Great Guns, Infantry Tactics, Field-Artillery, Boat-Howitzers, Mortar-practice, Marine Engines, Signals, Fencing, Boxing.

Marine Engines, Fabrication and Designing of Machinery, Mechanical Drawing, Naval Architecture, Mechanics, Light, Heat, Physical Measurements, Astronomy, Spanish, Public Law. Practical instruction in the use of tools, Marine Engines, Great Guns, Infantry Tactics, Field-Artillery, Signals, Fencing, Boxing.

108. The daily recitations shall take place according to the programme of studies prepared by the Academic Board.

109. Advanced courses in any branch of study taught at the Academy may be established by the Academic Board, with the approval of the Secretary of the Navy. Such advanced courses shall be elective, but shall be open only to Cadets whose standing shows marked ability or aptitude in the branch of study.

XVI.—EXAMINATIONS.

110. The semi-annual examination shall be held in the last week of the first term, and the programme shall be published by January 15.

111. Examinations on the work of the first term shall be held in all branches completed at that time.

Examination may be held in other branches as directed by the Academic Board.

112. The annual examination shall begin on June 10, and end on June 20, and the programme shall be published by June 1.

113. Examinations shall be held in all branches not completed at the end of the first term, unless otherwise determined by the Academic Board.

114. There shall be a competitive company-drill at some time during the annual examination, at which the judges shall be designated by the Superintendent, and a prize-flag shall be awarded to the best-drilled company. This flag shall be kept at the Academy, and the name of the captain of the winning company shall be inscribed on the staff.

115. Dress-parade shall take place daily during the annual examination, weather permitting.

116. The Secretary of the Navy will, when expedient, annually invite not less than seven persons, as a board of visitors at the Academy during the annual examination, to witness the examination and report on the discipline and management of the Academy.

117. No semi-annual or annual examination shall continue for more than five hours at a time, and no semi-monthly or monthly examination for more than two and a half hours.

118. Semi-monthly and monthly examinations shall be written, and other examinations may be either written or oral, or both. All oral examinations shall be conducted in the presence of the Head of the Department.

119. At the semi-annual and annual examinations each paper shall be marked by two instructors.

120. Recitations and other Academic exercises shall be suspended during the time of the semi-annual and annual examinations, unless otherwise directed by the Academic Board.

121. During the examinations, lectures, and theme exercises of a class, all members of the class on duty as Officers of the Day, or Superintendents of Floor or Building, shall be relieved and shall attend the examination, lecture, or exercise.

122. Cadets who are absent from an examination from any cause shall make it up as soon as possible.

123. The same rule shall apply to themes, and to all other written exercises.

124. In cases of absence from a semi-monthly or monthly examination, Cadets shall hold themselves in readiness for examination immediately after the expiration of their excuse without special notification.

125. In cases of absence from a semi-annual or annual examination, Cadets shall be examined at such times as the Academic Board may determine.

126. Cadets shall be allowed to leave an examination-room before finishing their work only in case of necessity. If absent longer than ten minutes (except in case of illness) no account shall be taken of their work; but they shall be required to pass a new examination at the earliest convenient time.

127. Cadets who ave finished their work shall be allowed to leave the examination-room in detachments of not less than seven, and over each of these divisions the senior instructor in charge shall appoint a section-leader, who shall be responsible for his section while marching through the grounds.

128. No Cadet shall be allowed to graduate, or pass from a lower to a higher class, until he has passed a physical examination, conducted by the Senior Medical Officer of the Academy.

129. Cadets shall at all times during the Academic course be subject to examination in the elementary branches.

XVII.—MARKS.

130. The scale of marks for recitation and exercises shall range from 4 to 0. A mark of 4 shall indicate thoroughness; 0, a total failure; and the intermediate numbers shall, as far as possible, represent absolute values.

131. A mark of 2.5 shall represent the minimum of proficiency; and Cadets whose final average for the term or year in any branch falls below that number shall be reported to the Academic Board as deficient in that branch.

132. Any Cadet absent without proper authority from a recitation, examination, or exercise, shall receive 0 as his mark.

133. Any Cadet who, at an examination, recitation, or exercise, or in the preparation of a theme, shall copy from another, or shall receive any unauthorized assistance, written, printed, or oral, or shall attempt to obtain such assistance, or shall be found with any unauthorized printed or written matter in his possession relating to the subject of the recitation or exercise, shall receive 0 as his mark for such exercise, and shall be punished as the Superintendent may direct, for such unfair and unworthy conduct.

134. In all cases, except those mentioned in Arts. 132 and 133, where 0 is given as a mark, the instructor giving the mark should inform the Cadet of the fact.

135. Marks given in recitation before the first Monday of the first term shall go on to the next week.

136. During the intermission, from the end of the last month of the second term to the beginning of the annual examination, no marks shall be given in recitations.

137. Unless otherwise directed by the Academic Board, averages shall be computed in the following manner: Whenever a Cadet shall receive more than one mark during the week in any branch, the arithmetical mean of such marks shall constitute his weekly average in that branch. The mean of the weekly averages in any month combined with the examination-mark, if monthly examinations are held, shall constitute the monthly average. The mean of the monthly averages for the term or year, combined with the semi-annual or annual examination-marks, shall constitute the final average for the term or year.

138. Weekly averages shall be recorded to the nearest tenth, all other averages to the nearest hundredth.

139. When the weekly mark of any Cadet consists of a mark for a single recitation, in a branch which has more than one recitation per week, the mark shall be considered as having one-half the weight of the average for any other week.

140. If two members of a class have the same average in any branch for the month, term, or year, they shall receive the same class-number and their names shall be placed alphabetically.

141. In marking examination-papers or other written exercises, in all departments, some account shall be taken of the form, language, and spelling, as well as of the subject-matter, and cases of gross carelessness shall be reported to the Academic Board.

142. In the case of Cadets who take an elective course in any branch, the final mark in that branch shall be determined by adding to the final mark received in the required course one-fifth of the amount by which the final mark in the elective course exceeds 2.50.

XVIII.—MERIT-ROLLS.

143. At every annual examination the Academic Board shall form a merit-roll of each class in the following manner:

144. The final average of each Cadet, in each branch for which a coefficient is assigned in the table of coefficients, shall be multiplied by such coefficient, and the sum of the products, after making the deduction for conduct, shall be the final multiple for the year.

145. The names of those Cadets who have not been found deficient by the Academic Board shall be arranged according to the final multiple, the highest multiple being placed first on the list and the others in their order. After these names, shall follow the names of those Cadets who may have been found deficient, arranged in the same manner; but no class-number shall be assigned to any Cadet who has been found deficient.

146. The merit-roll of the graduating class shall contain in addition a list of the class arranged in order of merit according to the graduating multiple, made up by adding together the final multiples for the four years.

147. Merit-rolls sent to the Navy Department shall contain only the names of Cadets passed by the Academic Board.

148. In the case of a Cadet turned back to go over the course of any year, his final multiple for the course shall be made up from the sum of the final multiples of the years in which he passed.

149. In the case of a Cadet advanced to any class without going over the course of the previous year, the final multiple for that year shall be made up by regarding his examination-averages as yearly averages.

150. Cadets who attain 85 per cent. of the multiple in any year shall be distinguished by a star affixed to their names on the merit-rolls.

XIX.—PRACTICE CRUISE.

151. There shall be attached to the Academy suitable vessels equipped and kept in order for sea-service and gunnery-practice.

152. There shall be attached to the practice-ship such officers and men as may be required to keep the vessel in order, and for the practical instruction of the Cadets in seamanship, navigation, and gunnery.

153. The Cadets of the classes not yet graduated shall be embarked, immediately after the June examination, on board the practice-ships to perform such cruise as the Secretary of the Navy may direct.

154. The practice-ships in which the Cadet-Midshipmen are thus embarked shall be commanded by the Commandant of Cadets under general instructions from the Superintendent. The Cadet-Midshipmen shall be required to perform such duties connected with practical seamanship, naval gunnery, practical navigation, and other professional subjects as the Commandant of Cadets may direct.

Their mess arrangements and supplies shall be subject to the control of the Superintendent, and, when aboard, of the Commandant of Cadets.

155. The vessel in which the Cadet-Engineers are embarked shall, during the summer, visit such founderies, mills, shops, and yards as may be designated by the Superintendent.

156. When the Cadets are to be embarked in practice-ships for a cruise, such officers and instructors, belonging to the Academy, shall be ordered to her as the Secretary of the Navy may deem advisable; and, while so embarked, they shall perform such duties of instruction, and as watch and division officers at quarters, according to their grades, as the commander of the ship may direct.

157. Cadets, when embarked in a practice-ship, shall be subject to all the regulations of the Academy which the commander of the practice squadron or ship may judge applicable.

XX.—REGISTER.

158. A Register of the Naval Academy shall be published annually as soon after October 1 as possible.

159. The Register shall contain the Academic Calendar; a list of the officers attached to the Academy; a list of Cadet-Officers and petty officers; alphabetical lists of classes corrected up to October 1, with the relative standing for the last year; a list of resignations, dismissals, and deaths; a list of Officers and Cadets attached to the practice-ships; the table of coefficients; the merit-rolls for the last year; the regulations governing the admission of candidates, and the papers set at the last examination for admission; the course of instruction and the programme of studies; and examination papers set during the previous year.

U. S. NAVAL ACADEMY,

Order, No. 98.   *September 18, 1877.*

By authority of the Navy Department, paragraph 160 of the Régulations of the Naval Academy, has been amended by the following addition :—

"He (the Superintendent) may appoint one Cadet Passed Assistant Engineer with the rank of Cadet Lieutenant.

One Cadet Assistant Engineer; with the relative rank of Cadet Master.

One Cadet Assistant Engineer, with the relative rank of Cadet Ensign.

Four Cadet Machinists, with the relative rank of First Captain of Gun.

Four Cadet Machinists, with the relative rank of Second Captain of Gun."

By the same authority, paragraph 161, of the Naval Academy Regulations has also been amended by adding to it the following words :—

"The Cadet Engineers of the First Class shall form an Engineer Division, under the command of the Cadet Passed Assistant Engineer, to be placed at the center of the battalion, when forming with it. This division shall be drilled in Engineering under the general direction of the Head of the Department of Steam Engineering, whenever the battalion shall be drilled in Artillery or Infantry Tactics, under the general direction of the Head of the Department of Gunnery."

C. R. P. RODGERS,
Rear-Admiral, Superintendent

PART II.—INTERIOR DISCIPLINE.

CADET ORGANIZATION.

160. The Superintendent shall appoint (from the First Class, as far as practicable) the following Cadet-Officers, who shall hold their positions during good behavior and efficiency :

One Cadet Lieutenant-Commander.
Four Cadet Lieutenants.
Five Cadet Masters.
Four Cadet Ensigns, and Cadet petty officers comprising first and second Captains of guns' crews.

161. The Cadets shall be arranged in four divisions for great-gun exercise, the divisions containing an equal number of guns' crews. Each gun's crew shall be composed of sixteen men, distributed as nearly as possible among the several classes.

162. Each division shall constitute a battery for light-artillery drill, and a company for infantry drill, and shall be commanded by a Cadet Lieutenant, as Captain, with a Cadet Master and Cadet Ensign as the other commissioned officers, and Cadet petty officers as non-commissioned officers.

163. The guns' crews shall be divided into watches, the odd-numbered crews making the starboard-watch, and the even-numbered crews the port-watch. The watches shall be stationed as ship's company for exercises in seamanship.

164. For exercises in naval tactics, the boats' crews shall be arranged according to the quarter-bill.

165. The Cadet Lieutenant-Commander shall bear the same relation to the Cadet organization that an Executive Officer bears to a ship's company.

He shall be present at all general formations, and shall receive divisional reports, which shall be made through him to the Officer-in-Charge.

In the battalion organization he shall act as Lieutenant-Colonel.

166. One of the Cadet Masters shall be selected to act as Adjutant of the battalion. At all general formations he shall take his post opposite the right of the battalion, eight paces in rear of the file-closers, unless otherwise specially assigned.

167. The color company of the battalion shall be the one to which the prize-flag has been awarded at the competitive drill of the preceding year.

CONDUCT.

168. The laws for the government of the Navy, and the Navy Regulations, as far as applicable, shall be observed by all persons attached to the Academy.

169. Cadets guilty of any of the following offenses shall be dismissed the service, or otherwise punished, as a Court-Martial, the Secretary of the Navy, or the Superintendent may direct:

Intoxication; using or bringing within the Academic limits, or having in possession, any wine or spirituous or fermented liquor; going beyond the Academic limits without permission; using profane or obscene language; lying or prevarication; unbecoming behavior in Chapel or on Sunday; playing cards, chess, backgammon, or any game of chance, or bringing within the Academic limits any cards, dice, or other implements used in such games; insulting or offering violence to a watchman or other person on duty; using reproachful or provoking language or gestures toward another Cadet, or traducing or defaming another; causing publications, or submitting articles for publication, or corresponding with official persons in regard to transactions at the Naval Academy; the persistent use of tobacco, or the introduction of it within the Academic limits; feigning illness or disability; copying from another Cadet, or receiving or attempting to receive unauthorized assistance at an examination, recitation, or exercise, or in the preparation of a theme, or having in possession at any exercise unauthorized printed or written matter relating to the subject of the exercise; refusing to take another Cadet into confinement, to any designated place, when ordered to do so by a person having competent authority; or failing to obey with promptness and precision.

170. The practice of molesting, annoying, ridiculing, maltreating, or assuming unauthorized authority over the new Cadets of the Fourth Class, known under the term hazing, running, &c., shall subject the older Cadets to prompt dismissal from the Naval Academy, as prescribed by the act of Congress and the orders of the Secretary of the Navy.

171. Demerits shall not be given as punishment, but as a record of misconduct.

172. A record shall be kept of punishments, and a separate record of offenses and demerits.

173. Whenever a Cadet of the First Class shall have 150 demerits in any Academic year; of the Second Class, 200; of the Third Class, 250; or of the Fourth Class, 300; his case shall be reported to the Navy Department, with such recommendations as the Academic Board may think proper. If a Cadet shall receive no demerits during one Academic month there shall be removed from the total number recorded against him 15 in the First Class, 20 in the Second Class, 25 in the Third Class, and 30 in the Fourth Class; if he receive six or less during one Academic month, his demerits for that month shall be removed; but, in such cases, no demerits shall be removed if the aggregate exceed those mentioned above, nor shall the removal be considered in making deductions for conduct from the final multiple.

174. The attention of Cadets is called to the misdemeanor-book, and to the number of demerits assigned therein for each offense.

175. No punishments, except the following, shall be inflicted, unless by order of the Secretary of the Navy:

1. Solitary confinement not exceeding seven days;
2. Coventry;
3. Public reprimand on parade, by written orders signed by the Superintendent;
4. Confinement under guard;
5. Confinement in quarters;
6. Deprivation of leave;
7. Deprivation of recreation;
8. Extra watch or guard duty and drill;
9. Imposition of extra duties;
10. Suspension;
11. Reduction of Cadet rank.

176. Removal from the service can be ordered only by the Secretary of the Navy.

177. All offenses shall be reported to the Superintendent, and no punishment shall be inflicted on a Cadet except by his order.

178. Every report against a Cadet shall be examined at once,

3

or dismissed; and, in any case, Cadets shall be allowed to make an explanation to the Superintendent.

179. No Cadet under suspension shall perform the duties of Cadet-Officers, Officer of the Day, Superintendent of Floor or Building, or Section-leader, or exercise command of any sort. No Cadet under suspension shall go to entertainments, or visit the house or office of any officer unless sent for. In case of business, he shall make known his object in writing; and he shall not apply for the usual indulgences granted Cadets.

A Cadet while in coventry will not be permitted to mess at the same table with Cadets in good standing, nor will he be allowed to visit the quarters of any officer or professor, or the room of any other Cadet, nor will any other Cadet enter the room of a Cadet in coventry except upon duty.

No Cadet in coventry will be given any responsible duty. The suspension of Cadet-Officers and petty officers will, in addition to the above, include the restrictions of article 182.

180. The usual studies shall not be discontinued by Cadets undergoing any of the above punishments, except the first; but when under confinement they shall not attend recitation or drills.

181. Deprivation of recreation shall not be for a longer time than twenty days, nor confinement in guard-room longer than one week, without the express sanction of the Secretary of the Navy.

182. A Cadet under the punishment of deprivation of recreation shall not leave his room except during the time absolutely necessary to attend religious services, recitations, meals, and drills, and to answer calls of nature.

183. Any breach of confinement will be regarded as a grave military offense.

184. No Cadet shall visit any hotel, restaurant, or other place of public entertainment without special permission from the Superintendent, or the Commandant of Cadets acting for him.

185. No Cadet shall contract debts without the sanction of the Superintendent.

186. No Cadet shall join any association within or without the Academy, nor shall any meeting be called for any purpose without permission.

187. All combinations are forbidden.

188. Answering for another Cadet at roll-call is an act of falsehood, and shall be punished accordingly.

189. No fire-arms or fire-works, or gunpowder in any form, shall be introduced or discharged by any Cadet within the Academic limits except when authorized.

190. No Cadet shall introduce any person into the mess-hall or quarters without permission, nor any improper character within the Academic limits.

191. No Cadet shall allow food to be prepared in his room, or give any entertainment therein.

192. No Cadet shall receive any book or take any periodical without permission from the Superintendent, and no permission shall be given for more than one periodical at a time, paid for in advance.

193. No Cadet shall exchange or sell any articles belonging to him, or give away or otherwise dispose of any text-books, note-books, or reference-books.

194. Any Cadet who shall marry, or who shall be found to be married, shall be dismissed the service.

195. Any Cadet who shall, when absent from the Academy, commit any disgraceful act, may be punished as if the act had been committed at the Academy.

196. Any Cadet in a responsible position, who becomes answerable for infractions of the regulations, will be required to answer all questions of his superior officer relating to the offense, and he may relieve himself of his responsibility by reporting the offender.

197. Unless public notice of misbehavior at the moment be deemed inexpedient, officers observing any impropriety of conduct on the part of a Cadet shall call his attention to the fact at the time.

UNIFORM OF CADETS.

198. Full dress: Jacket, waistcoat, trousers, cap with visor and cord, and white gloves.

199. Undress: Coat, waistcoat, trousers, and cap without visor.

200. Working dress: Canvas blouse and trousers, worn over undress.

201. Unless otherwise ordered the full dress shall be worn on Sunday; on liberty, or when visiting officers' quarters by special invitation; at dress-parade, at entertainments, and on special occasions: at other times the undress shall be worn.

202. The working-dress shall be worn at certain exercises, specified in general orders.

203. The undress-coat shall be worn buttoned, except at morning roll-call, when it shall be unbuttoned, and the full-dress jacket shall be buttoned whenever it is worn at drills and formations.

204. Overcoats, rain-coats, cap-covers, and overshoes shall be worn when specially ordered by the Commandant of Cadets. Cap-covers shall be worn over the cord.

205. White trousers and white caps shall be worn at such times as the Superintendent may direct.

206. All articles of clothing shall be marked with the owner's name, and shall conform to patterns at the Paymaster's store.

207. No part of one dress shall be worn with another except as provided for in the working-dress.

208. No cadet shall carry his hands in his pockets.

209. Cadet-Officers shall wear such badges of rank as the Superintendent may prescribe.

210. Cadet-Midshipmen shall wear a gold anchor embroidered on each end of the collar of their jackets one inch and a quarter in length. Cadet-Engineers shall wear silver oak-leaves, instead of an anchor.

211. Distinguished cadets of the First Class (those who attain 85 per cent. of the multiple in the preceding year) shall wear an embroidered gold star on the collar behind the corps-badge.

212. Cadets shall wear their hair closely cut; and no Cadet shall wear whiskers, beard, or moustaches.

213. Jack-knives with laniards attached, long enough to go around the neck, shall be worn by Cadet-Midshipmen at seamanship-drills.

214. Dressing-gowns shall only be worn in rooms, and there only after forenoon inspection.

215. All articles of citizens' clothing shall be turned in, marked with the owner's name, as soon as possible after admission or return from leave, and no Cadet shall, at any time, have any article of citizens' clothing in his possession.

DAILY ROUTINE.

216. From September 20 to November 10, and from March 20 to the close of the Academic year:

ON WEEK DAYS.

Morning gun-fire and reveille	6 00 a. m.
Morning roll-call and prayers	6.45 a. m.

Breakfast	7.00 a. m.
Sick-call	7.30 a. m.
Morning call to studies	7.56 a. m.
Call to first morning-recitation, (first period)	8.26 a. m.
Call to second morning-recitation, (first period)	9.26 a. m.
Recall, (first period)	10.26 a. m.
Call to third morning-recitation, (second period)	10.41 a. m.
Call to fourth morning-recitation, (second period)	11.41 a. m.
Recall, (second period)	12.45 p. m.
Dinner-formation	12.55 p. m.
Call to first afternoon-recitation, (third period)	1.56 p. m.
Call to second afternoon-recitation (third period)	2.56 p. m.
Recall, (third period)	3.56 p. m.
Call to drill	4.05 p. m.
Preparatory recall	5.10 p. m.
Recall	5.15 p. m.
Call to dress-parade on Tuesday and Thursday	5.50 p. m.
Evening roll-call and parade before supper, September 20 to October 20, and April 20 to end of term	6.30 p. m.
October 20 to November 10, and March 20 to April 20	6.00 p. m.
Call to exercises in gymnasium fifteen minutes after supper.	
Call to evening studies	7.30 or 8 p. m.
(As directed by the Superintendent.)	
Gun-fire and tattoo	9.30 p. m.
Warning-roll	9.55 p. m.
Taps	10.00 p. m.
Saturday forenoon drill-call	10.35 a. m.

From November 10 to March 20, the following changes will be made in the routine:

Morning gun-fire and reveille	6.15 a. m.
Morning roll-call and prayers	7.00 a. m.
Breakfast	7.15 a. m.
Sick-call	7.45 a. m.
Evening roll-call and parade before supper	5.30 p. m.

ON SUNDAY, THROUGHOUT THE YEAR.

217. Morning gun-fire and reveille	6.30 or 6.45 a. m.
Morning roll-call and prayers	7.15 or 7.30 a. m.

Breakfast	7.30 or 7.45 a.m.
Sick-call	8.00 or 8.15 a.m.
Church-call, first Sunday in the month	10.26 a.m.
Church-call, other Sundays	10.40 a.m.
Dinner-formation	12.55 p.m.
Call to afternoon meditation	2.56 p.m.
Recall	3.56 p.m.
Evening roll-call and parade before supper	5.30 or 6.00 p.m.
Retreat-call	7.30 or 8.00 p.m.
Gun-fire and tattoo	9.30 p.m.
Warning-roll	9.55 p.m.
Taps	10.00 p.m.

218. Cadets shall rise promptly at morning gun-fire, dress without delay, make up their beds, and arrange their rooms in such manner as may be prescribed by the Commandant of Cadets.

219. The daily report of delinquencies involving demerits shall be read at morning roll-call.

220. The detail of Cadets to serve on the next day as Officer of the Day, and Superintendent of Floors and Buildings, shall be read at dinner-formation.

221. The day shall be divided for purposes of study and recitation into three periods, one of which shall be in the afternoon.

222. Study-hours shall last from the morning call to studies till the end of the second period ; from the call to afternoon-recitations till the end of the third period, and from the evening call to studies till gun-fire. Study-hours on Saturday shall end at 10.26 a.m.

223. The bugle shall sound the call for studies and recitations.

224. A drill shall take place on every day except Sunday, when the weather permits, immediately after the last recitation.

225. There shall be a dress-parade, on Tuesday and Thursday, during such periods of the year as the Superintendent may direct.

226. An inspection-parade shall take place, at church-formation on Sunday morning, after which the Cadets shall march to the chapel. On the first Sunday in every month, immediately after inspection, the Articles for the better government of the Navy shall be read, all the Naval officers attached to the Academy being present.

227. If the drum or gong sound to quarters at night, or at any times other than those specified, it shall be a signal for the Cadets to assemble as for drill, and await orders.

228. Cadets shall repair promptly to their rooms at warning-roll, and they shall turn in at taps.

229. The daily routine of studies, recitations, and exercises shall not be interrupted by extra parades or exercises on account of the presence of visitors, except by order of the Secretary of the Navy.

XXV.—OFFICIAL INTERCOURSE.

230. All communications to the Navy Department from persons connected with the Academy shall be made through the Superintendent, whose duty it shall be to forward them, with such comments as he may think proper.

231. Cadets wishing to address the Superintendent officially shall first obtain permission of the Commandant of Cadets.

232. Cadets wishing personal interviews with the Superintendent can have them on any day, Sunday excepted, when not engaged in their studies or recitations, between the hours of noon and 1 p. m. All business they may have with him shall be transacted at his office, and not at his quarters.

233. Written communications from Cadets to the Superintendent shall be forwarded through the Commandant of Cadets.

234. Cadets having cause of complaint against any person connected with the Academy may make it known to the Superintendent through the Commandant of Cadets.

235. Cadets having business with the Commandant of Cadets shall apply to the Officer-in-Charge for permission to visit his office, stating the nature of their business.

236. During recreation-hours Cadets may visit the library and officers' quarters, and, when their duties require, the Treasurer's and Secretary's offices, dispensary, and store; and they shall not visit these places at any other times except by permission of the Commandant of Cadets.

237. Cadets shall not go to the house or office of any officer to make a complaint or request in greater numbers than three at a time, and then only after obtaining permission from the Superintendent through the Commandant of Cadets.

238. No Cadet shall visit the guard-house, or the office of the Commandant of Cadets, or of the Officer-in-Charge except on duty.

239. No Cadet shall address an officer on the subject of marks without permission from the Superintendent.

240. No Cadet shall address an officer or Cadet who has reported a delinquency on the subject of such report, without permission from the Superintendent, and officers and Cadets shall not converse with offenders on the subject of such reports without permission.

241. All orders coming through an Officer of the Day, Superintendent of Floor or Building, or Cadet-Officer or petty officer, shall be considered as official and obeyed accordingly.

242. A message conveyed to an officer or Cadet by a messenger of the Superintendent or Commandant of Cadets, requiring his attendance, or the sending of any book or paper, or answer to a communication, shall be considered as emanating properly.

243. In passing or meeting, all officers, Naval, Civil, and Cadets, shall observe the customary Naval salute, the junior being the first to extend it.

XXVI.—RELIGIOUS SERVICE.

244. Prayers shall be said by the Chaplain daily, except on Sunday, immediately after morning roll-call.

245. Divine service shall be held on Sunday morning in the chapel, at which the attendance of Cadets is required.

246. Cadets shall occupy the seats assigned them, and shall comply with the forms of divine service.

247. Cadets belonging to the choir shall report to the Officer-in-Charge on Sunday at 10 a. m. for inspection.

248. Cadets may attend afternoon or evening service in the chapel. They shall not be required to march there, or to sit in their regular seats, but they shall register their names at the office of the Officer-in-Charge, going and returning. If the service is during meditation-hour, or any part thereof, they shall go directly to and from the chapel, returning to their quarters immediately after the close of the service.

249. Cadets attending evening service in the chapel shall return directly to their quarters. They may be allowed to escort ladies from the chapel, but not beyond the Academic limits, nor shall they enter any house on returning, nor delay at the door.

250. Permission to attend service permanently in the city of Annapolis shall be granted only on the written request of the parent or guardian. Church-parties shall fall out of ranks after inspection, and form and march to and from church in charge of their respective leaders, who shall report their return to the Officer-in-Charge. Leaders of church-parties shall be responsible for the conduct of parties in their charge, and shall report misdemeanors.

251. Cadets belonging to church-parties attending service in the city, who wish to attend afternoon service in the city, shall register their names, and report to the Officer-in-Charge, going and returning.

252. Cadets shall observe the Lord's Day with proper decorum.

XXVII.—HOSPITAL.

253. Lists of Cadets unfitted for duty by illness shall be sent daily from the hospital to the Commandant of Cadets.

254. The sick-list shall contain the names of Cadets excused from all recitations, drills, and formations.

255. The excused-list shall contain the names of Cadets excused only from drills and the corresponding formations.

256. No Cadet shall be excused from duty on the plea of sickness unless his name is put on the list by the Medical Officer.

257. All the sick not in the hospital who are able to attend shall report to the Medical Officer at sick-call, and those already on the sick or excused list shall report daily until discharged by him.

258. Cadets whose names are removed from the sick-list at the morning sick-call shall attend their regular recitations on that day, but shall be excused from reciting during the first period, upon informing the Instructor of the fact.

259. Cadets requiring medical attendance at other times than the regular sick-call shall report the fact to the Officer-in-Charge, who shall send them to the Medical Officer on duty, for examination.

260. No Cadet on the sick or excused list shall leave the Academic limits unless upon recommendation of the Senior Medical Officer, approved by the Superintendent; nor shall he leave his room, except for a call of nature, during any drill or formation from which he shall have been excused by the Surgeon's list.

261. No Cadet on the sick-list shall leave his room except to take exercise, and then only at such times as the Medical Officer may have prescribed.

262. No patient in the hospital shall exercise any authority over the apothecary, nurse, or attendant; but all cases of neglect on the part of employés shall be reported to the Medical Officer.

263. No Cadet shall visit a patient in the hospital without a written permission signed by the Senior Medical Officer and approved by the Superintendent; nor shall any other person visit a patient without permission of the Senior Medical Officer.

264. The sick in the hospital shall conform to the directions of the Medical Officer, and to all police regulations of the hospital.

265. No person shall be employed in the hospital without the approval of the Superintendent.

XXVIII.—LIBRARY.

266. The library shall be under the supervision of a committee composed of the Librarian, and four members of the Academic Board designated by the Superintendent.

267. The committee shall recommend the purchase of books for the library, and shall have charge of the arrangement of books and catalogues, and of the exchange and disposal of duplicates and undesirable books, subject to the Superintendent.

268. The Librarian, or one of his assistants, shall be in attendance at the library for the purposes of receiving and delivering books at such times as the Superintendent may direct.

269. No persons except officers connected with the Academy and Cadets of the First and of the Second Class, shall draw books from the library without permission from the Superintendent.

270. No book or periodical shall be drawn from the library without the knowledge and presence of the Librarian or one of his assistants, and an entry thereof shall be made in all cases.

271. No person shall lend any book or periodical belonging to the library.

272. No person shall, without special permission from the Superintendent, keep any book more than one month, or a number of any periodical more than one week, or have in his possession at the same time more than four volumes, (each number of a periodical being in this respect, regarded as a volume,) except the Heads of Departments, who shall be allowed such books as are required in the work of their departments.

273. No Cadet shall keep any book longer than one week without renewal, or have in his possession more than one volume at a time.

274. Any book returned within the prescribed time may be taken out anew by the same person, if not called for by another in the mean time.

275. Persons leaving the Academy for a longer time than seven days shall return all books belonging to the library before departure.

276. All books belonging to the library shall be returned before the beginning of the annual examination, and no books shall be issued during that examination.

277. No number of a periodical shall be taken from the library until it has been at least fifteen days therein, or until the receipt of the next succeeding number.

278. Damage done to any book or periodical shall be charged against the person to whom it was issued, and no person shall draw books against whom such charge remains standing.

279. No unbound numbers of periodicals, or any rare or costly work, shall be issued to Cadets.

280. Any Cadet who shall willfully mutilate any book, number of a periodical, or paper, or who shall, without proper authority, remove from the library any book, periodical, or paper, shall be dismissed the service or otherwise severely punished.

XXIX.—GYMNASIUM.

281. Cadets may use the gymnasium, bowling-alley, and pistol-gallery, during recreation-hours; no other person shall use them during these hours.

282. Cadets of the Fourth Class are forbidden to go to the gymnasium except at the prescribed exercises in fencing and dancing, and at entertainments.

283. No exercise shall be allowed in the gymnasium during the half hour after each meal.

284. The Fourth Class shall form at 7.30 p. m. on Friday, and be marched to the gymnasium, to receive instruction in dancing until 9 p. m.

285. Cadets of the other classes wishing to take lessons in dancing shall put their names on the list in the office of the Officer-in-Charge, and proceed to the gymnasium at 6.30 p. m.

286. Cadets breaking foils shall note the fact without delay in the book kept at the gymnasium for that purpose.

XXX.—STORE.

287. Cadets in need of such articles as the Store-keeper may be authorized to furnish, may send in requisitions once a month, at such times as the Commandant of Cadets may direct. Such requisitions shall be neatly entered in the requisition-books, and the columns on the inside of the covers shall be kept filled out with the articles received and on hand.

288. Requisition-books shall be sent to the office of the Commandant of Cadets by 9 a. m. of the day following that on which they are issued. Upon his approval, they will be sent to the Store-keeper, who shall furnish the articles required and approved, at such times as the Cadets may be sent to the store. No article shall be issued after the 25th day of the month.

289. After the requisitions are served they shall be entered, with the prices extended, in the pass-books of the Cadets, by the Store-keeper's clerk, and the pass-books shall be sent to the office of the Commandant of Cadets, from which they shall be issued to the Cadets for inspection. If found correct upon examination, they shall be certified and signed by the owner, and returned to the Commandant's Office. If incorrect, the Cadet shall make a report accordingly.

290. No disorderly conduct, or going behind the counter, shall be allowed at the store.

XXXI.—GROUNDS.

291. The grounds and buildings of the Academy shall be under the special charge of the Senior Aid to the Superintendent.

292. The Academic limits include the grounds within the walls, the wharves, and the public ships moored alongside.

293. No person shall mark, deface, or injure in any way, the buildings, walls, trees, or other public property within the Academic limits, or post any placard or notice except by authority. Injury to public property shall be made good by the person causing it.

294. No person shall discharge any fire-arm or fire-works within the grounds without permission from the Superintendent, or throw stones or missiles of any kind in the vicinity of the public buildings, or make a disturbance of any kind within the Academic limits.

295. No smoking shall be allowed in the grounds during the session, or in the public buildings, except the Officers' mess-hall and quarters.

296. Families of officers and all other persons residing within the Academic limits, are required to observe such regulations as may be established for the preservation of public property; and officers shall enjoin this rule upon persons under their control or in their employ.

297. No children shall be allowed in or about the public buildings, and no servants, unless employed there, or sent there by proper authority.

298. No general passes shall be given by officers.

299. No Cadets shall enter the shell-boat house unless they own a boat there or belong to a crew.

300. Cadets passing in or out of the grounds shall use the upper gate.

XXXII.—CADETS' QUARTERS.

301. The rooms of Cadets shall be ready for inspection at any time from half an hour after reveille until the call to evening studies, arranged in the following manner:

The floors carefully swept, and free from spots, with a rug in front of the bed.

The walls free from cobwebs.

Steam-heaters and gas-fixtures clean.

Mantel-pieces dusted, and free from articles not connected with studies.

Wardrobes neatly arranged, and doors closed and locked except at inspection, when they shall be opened by the owner, whose name shall be placed on the centre of the wardrobe, above the doors.

Beds about one foot from the wall, with the occupant's name on the head-rail, and neatly made, with sides and lower end of coverlet tucked under lower mattress.

Tables directly under the gas-pendant, with only such books as are in use at the time; papers neatly arranged, and inkstand in the centre.

Chairs, one for each occupant, placed beside the table when not in use.

Washstands placed against the wall and kept clean, with washing-furniture in place, and nothing else on the washstand.

Towels neatly folded and hung upon the racks.

One bucket on each side of the washstand, with cover beside it.
Foot-tubs kept empty and clean, on the lower shelf of the wash-stand.

Looking-glass over the washstand, or on the mantel-piece.

Broom in corner near the washstand.

Clothes and slippers kept in wardrobes.

Dressing-gowns, when not in use, neatly folded and placed on the foot of the bed.

Shoes neatly blacked, and arranged under the foot of the bed.

Books neatly arranged on the mantel-piece, or on the top of the wardrobe if there is no mantel-piece, with the backs outward.

302. No unauthorized articles shall be allowed in the rooms.

303. No curtains shall be hung, or nails driven into walls or woodwork, nor shall the walls be marked or defaced.

304. No map, picture, or piece of writing, except as directed, shall be affixed to the walls.

305. Chairs, coverlets, table-cloths, and rugs shall conform to the prescribed pattern.

306. Cadets are forbidden to sit at the windows, or on the beds, or to throw anything from the windows or into the corridor.

307. Transom-windows shall be kept open, and the cleats shall not be interfered with.

308. Lights shall be burned only when necessary; they shall always be turned low in the absence of both occupants of the room; they shall be put out at taps, and no light shall be burned during the night except by authority. Only one light shall be kept burning out of study-hours.

309. The table of "hours of recitation," of each Cadet, shall be posted on the inside of the door, in the middle of the panels, and at the same height.

A copy of special regulations for quarters shall be posted below the "hours of recitation."

310. Cadets shall rise and remain standing and uncovered when the Officer-in-Charge, Officer of the Day, or Superintendent of the Floor or Building enters the room.

311. On Sunday, Cadets shall be in their rooms, in full dress, ready to receive the Officer-in-Charge, at 9.30 a. m., and they shall remain in their quarters until the end of the inspection.

312. During study-hours no Cadet shall visit another, or absent himself from his room unnecessarily.

313. Cadets leaving their rooms during study-hours on a necessary occasion shall report their departure and return to the Superintendent of the Floor or Building, and shall be absent as short a time as possible. If the absence is longer than 15 minutes, the Superintendent shall report the fact to the Officer-in-Charge.

314. Cadets shall use the main entrance in entering and leaving the new quarters, unless otherwise ordered.

315. In pleasant weather the route to the water-closets of the new quarters shall be by the central staircase to the rear door, opposite the front entrance, and thence by the side-walk. In bad weather, the route shall be by the central staircase to the first floor, thence to northeast end of the building and northeast entrance.

316. During the washing of a room, the Officer-in-Charge may permit the occupant to visit another room until his own can be occupied.

317. Cadets shall have their clothes and wash-book ready for the laundress before 7 a. m. on Monday.

318. Shoes shall be put inside the room-door at night, to be taken and blacked by the servants.

319. No Cadet shall play upon any musical instrument on Sunday, or in study-hours on any other day ; nor sit up after taps ; nor remove from the room assigned him, nor enter unoccupied rooms, unless specially ordered ; nor send out an attendant for any purpose.

320. Loud talking and boisterous conduct in the rooms or corridors are forbidden.

321. No person shall enter the Cadets' room during study-hours, except on duty, without permission from the Superintendent.

XXXIII.—MESS-HALL.

322. The Officer-in-Charge at the new quarters shall preside at meals, and shall have charge of the police of the mess-hall, assisted by the Cadet-Officers and petty officers.

323. He shall inspect the mess-hall and servants daily, at 12.30 p. m.

324. At meals he shall enter the hall before the Cadets, and he shall make an inspection after they have left the hall.

325. A table shall be arranged at which he shall inspect the quality and preparation of the provisions.

326. A seat at meals shall be assigned to each Cadet, which he shall not change unless ordered by the Officer-in-Charge.

327. When the Cadets have entered the hall before a meal, the Officer-in-Charge shall give the order, "Seats!" Thirty minutes shall be allowed for breakfast and for supper, and forty minutes for dinner. At the end of this time, the Officer-in-Charge shall give the order, "Rise!" the crews shall be marched from the hall, and the doors shall be closed.

328. Captains of crews will see that chairs are not moved back, before and after meals, until the order is given.

329. No Cadet shall leave the mess-hall without permission, nor by any but the main door.

330. Cadets shall dress with care for meals.

331. Loud talking at the mess-table, or reading, or carrying books or newspapers into the mess-hall, is forbidden.

332. The inspecting officer and his aids shall report any slovenliness, wastefulness, or breach of decorum.

333. No article of food or furniture shall be taken from the mess-hall.

334. No articles of food or furniture shall be introduced into the mess-hall except those provided by the Commissary.

335. No extra meals shall be served in the mess-hall except by permission of the Superintendent; and no meal shall be served in rooms except in case of illness, and then only by direction of the Medical Officer, and in strict accordance with the diet-list prescribed by him.

336. Cadets absent on leave for a week or more, on giving notice of their intended absence to the Commissary, shall receive credit on the mess-account for the time of absence.

337. Complaints in regard to the quantity or quality of provisions, the manner of cooking, negligence of Commissary, or inattention of servants, may be made to the inspecting officer, who shall, if necessary, report them to the Superintendent.

XXXIV.—OFFICER-IN-CHARGE.

338. The Assistant Instructors in the Department of Seamanship, and of Ordnance and Gunnery, shall perform in succession the duty of Officer-in-Charge at their respective buildings, from 8 a. m. until 10 p. m.

339. The duty from 10 p. m. until 8 a. m. shall be performed by officers detailed for that purpose.

340. The lists of officers detailed for duty shall be kept posted in both offices. Officers shall keep themselves informed of their duty without notification.

341. The Officer-in-Charge shall have similar duties and responsibilities with the Executive Officer on board ship, under the Commandant of Cadets.

342. He shall wear a sword and white gloves when on duty, except in the office, and such other uniform as the Superintendent may prescribe.

343. He shall use courtesy in his official intercourse with Cadets, and shall avoid wounding their feelings; and he shall advise and direct them, when it may seem necessary.

344. He shall enforce all regulations, and use every endeavor to detect offenses.

345. He shall be charged with the cleanliness of buildings and servants under his care.

346. He shall attend formations, as far as possible, and shall preserve order.

347. He shall inspect the battalion at morning roll-call; if possible, during the time occupied in reading the report.

348. He shall make an inspection of Cadets' rooms at 10 a. m. on week days, and at 9.30 a. m. on Sunday, and at other times at discretion.

349. Military etiquette shall govern the exchange of salutations between a Cadet and his superior officer at inspection of quarters.

350. The Officer-in-Charge shall regulate the temperature of the Cadets' rooms, and shall see that they are not kept unnecessarily warm.

351. He shall inspect all parts of the quarters under his charge before turning in, guarding specially against fire.

352. No permission shall be granted to sit up after taps, or to burn lights, except in case of illness, or some extraordinary circumstance.

353. The Officer-in-Charge shall not make nor permit to be made, on the daily conduct-report, scandalous or unusual reports against Cadets. Such reports must be special and direct to the Commandant of Cadets.

4

354. He shall see that Cadets are not reported for offenses of which they are not guilty, or guilty in a less degree than charged.

355. Resignations and dismissals shall be read at parade before being delivered.

356. No order shall be read at parade or posted unless signed by the Superintendent, or the Commandant of Cadets.

357. Instructors' reports, sick-lists, and details shall be kept on file.

358. The Officer-in-Charge shall examine and sign the journal before it is sent to the Superintendent.

359. He shall pass to his relief the names of Cadets under punishment and the character of the punishment.

360. The Officer-in-Charge at the old quarters shall, from time to time, visit the grounds in that neighborhood. He shall attend hops and dancing-lessons, and shall preside at the gymnasium at other times, as may be ordered.

361. He shall have charge of the colors of the flag-staff. The flag-ship shall be the guide in hoisting and hauling down ; but the colors shall always be hauled down in bad weather, or shall not be hoisted.

XXXV.—OFFICER OF THE DAY.

362. At dinner-formation two Cadet-Midshipmen of the First Class shall be detailed for duty as Officers of the Day, at the old and the new quarters, beginning on the day following at 7.30 p. m., and continuing twenty-four hours.

363. The Officer of the Day shall wear a sword and white gloves during his tour of duty, except while at meals.

364. He shall receive with courtesy and treat with attention all strangers and citizens who may visit the Academy and apply to him for information.

365. He shall at all times enforce the regulations, and shall assume the duties of the Officer-in-Charge in the absence of the latter.

366. He shall not attend drills or recitations during his tour of duty; but shall be present at roll-calls and mess-formations ; and he shall superintend at section-formations, seek absentees not accounted for, order them to go to the proper room, and report all delinquencies. He may study the lesson of the day, but reading or writing for other purposes is forbidden.

367. He shall keep notes of new orders, and inspect the memorandum-book to take notice of any orders which may have been issued since his last tour of duty; and he shall cause all the signals to be sounded.

368. He shall have control of the watchman, or non-commissioned officer, on duty at the new quarters, and shall see that he secures the fires and extinguishes the lights at 10 p. m.

369. He shall prepare the daily conduct report, copying it neatly and without erasures or interlineations from the rough reports; the names shall be arranged alphabetically, with the number of the class annexed to each name, and the rank prefixed to the name of the reporting officer or Cadet-Officer.

370. Reports and excuses, arranged in the order of the names on the conduct-report, and requests that require immediate attention, shall be ready for examination by 8.45 a. m.

371. The Officer of the Day shall enter the names of all Cadets going on and returning from liberty in the liberty-book, and note exactly the time of going and return.

372. He shall enter in the journal the date, the state of the weather, and direction of the wind throughout the day; the readings of the barometer and thermometer; the afternoon drill and its character; and the following events whenever they may occur: target practice, with a note of the projectiles used; the visits of public functionaries of high rank or position, and the ceremonies attending their reception; the beginning, continuance, and end of semi-annual and annual examinations; dismissals and resignations; cases of suspension and restoration to duty; confinement and release of Cadets, and other incidents of importance.

373. The record shall be signed by the Officer of the Day, and be carried by his successor to the office of the Superintendent for inspection by 9 a. m. on the next day.

374. The Officer of the Day shall be held responsible if the journal is defaced.

375. No passes shall be issued by the Officer of the Day; if a pass is required during the absence of the Officer-in-Charge, it shall be sent to him for signature.

376. The Officer of the Day shall not visit any of the Cadets' rooms except on duty.

377. He shall prevent loitering about his desk or elsewhere during his tour.

378. He shall be responsible during his tour for Cadets committed to the guard-house. Such Cadets shall be regarded as in his custody, and at the close of his tour he shall visit the rooms in which they are confined and shall report their presence or absence to the Officer-in-Charge.

379. The Officer of the Day at the old quarters shall march to the "Santee" such Cadets as are directed to be confined there.

380. *Routine of duty:* Immediately after coming on duty, the Officer of the Day shall inspect the lower floor and arrange rough reports for the Officer-in-Charge.

At 8 p. m., record barometer and thermometer.

During the evening, copy daily conduct report and give it to the Officer-in-Charge.

At 10 p. m., receive the reports of Superintendents of Floors; visit the upper floors at warning-roll, and whenever it may be necessary to preserve order.

As soon after taps as possible, report concerning lights and receive permission to turn in.

Rise when called by the orderly, before reveille, and proceed to post.

Visit floors to see that Superintendents are ready to make their inspections at the proper time.

Return to post and see that the morning orders are ready for publication, and deliver them to the Cadet Lieutenant-Commander.

At morning roll-call attend the Officer-in-Charge while making his inspection.

Immediately after roll-call have the conduct-report posted.

At 8 a. m., take barometer and thermometer and inspect buglers.

On Saturday and Sunday, make out liberty and church list during the forenoon and take them to the Commandant of Cadets for approval.

At 9 a. m., take the journal to the Superintendent's office.

At noon, take barometer and thermometer.

At dinner formation, prepare the orders and deliver them to the Cadet Lieutenant-Commander to be published, and after formation submit them to the Officer-in-Charge before posting them.

At 4 p. m., take barometer and thermometer.

Prepare orders for publication at supper-formation.

After supper, muster gymnasium parties and write rough journal, submitting it to the Officer-in-Charge for approval.

At 7.30 p. m., conduct the relief over the lower floor and pass any orders that may have been received.

XXXVI.—SUPERINTENDENTS OF FLOORS OR BUILDINGS.

381. The Cadets occupying each floor, or building, shall be detailed to serve in turn as Superintendents.

382. Superintendents of Floors or Buildings shall wear white gloves while on duty.

383. The tour of duty shall begin at the call to evening studies, and last twenty-four hours.

384. The Superintendent of a Floor or Building shall see that all Cadets go to their rooms at warning roll.

385. At taps he shall inspect the rooms, to see that lights are out and occupants turned in, and he shall remain on his floor until the Officer of the Day receives his report and gives him permission to retire.

386. He shall report to the Officer-in-Charge for duty, twenty minutes before the beat to morning roll call.

387. He shall inspect his floor, or building, fifteen minutes before the beat to morning roll call, and at the close of his inspection report the names of delinquents to the Officer-in-Charge, being the last of those who attend formation to leave his floor or building.

388. Before 10 a. m. he shall inspect the rooms and see that they are in readiness for inspection by the Officer-in-Charge.

389. He shall hand in a written report, within half an hour after call to evening studies, of all offenses that may have come to his notice.

390. At the close of his tour he shall make an inspection of his corridor, or building, in company with his relief, and shall take note of any marks defacing the doors or walls.

391. He shall inspect the rooms in his charge immediately after the call to each period of study, or meditation hour, and report absences, at the close of his inspection, to the Officer-in-Charge.

392. He shall make frequent inspections of his floor or building, and shall be responsible for the preservation of order at all times.

393. Every occupied room over which he has charge shall be open to him for inspection at all hours of the day and night. He shall not knock upon the doors of rooms, but he shall conduct his inspections so as not to interrupt studies unnecessarily.

394. He shall take care that unoccupied rooms on his floor or building shall not be entered or used by Cadets, and that the doors are kept locked.

395. He shall preserve the public property in his charge.

396. He shall have charge of all formations on his floor, or in front of his building, and shall preserve order.

397. He shall attend drills and all general formations during his tour of duty, but shall not attend recitations.

398. He shall not have any conversation with Cadets except such as his duties may require.

399. He shall prevent loitering around his desk or elsewhere, and visiting on other floors or in other buildings.

400. He shall distribute the mail.

401. He may study the lessons of the day, but reading or writing for other purposes is forbidden.

XXXVII.—SUPERINTENDENTS OF ROOMS.

402. The Cadets occupying each room shall alternate weekly as Superintendent, unless otherwise directed by the Commandant of Cadets.

403. The Superintendent of a Room shall post his name in his room, above that of his room-mate, in such place and manner as the Commandant of Cadets may direct.

404. He shall be responsible for the general cleanliness of the room, and of such furniture as is used by both occupants in common, and for the observance of regulations in the room.

405. He shall be responsible for the preservation of all public property used in the room by both occupants, and shall see that the regulations about lights are obeyed.

406. He shall sweep out and prepare the room for early morning inspection. The sweepings from the rooms shall be put into the adjoining passage, from which they shall be removed at once by a servant.

407. When a room has but one occupant he shall have the duties and responsibilities of Superintendent.

408. When the Superintendent of a Room is on the sick-list, or acting as Superintendent of Floor or Building, or as Officer of the Day, his name shall be reversed, and his room-mate shall act in his place.

XXXVIII.—WATCHMEN AND MASTER-AT-ARMS.

409. The watchmen shall keep a watch upon all public property, and report any violations of regulations that come under their notice; and they shall light and put out the lamps in the grounds.

410. At least one watchman or non-commissioned officer shall remain in the recitation-hall, and in the lower corridor of the new quarters, during the absence of the Officer of the Day, at meals, or otherwise.

411. The watchman or non-commissioned officer on duty shall be under the orders of the Officer of the Day.

412. He shall visit all the floors every hour, and report any misconduct that may come to his notice to the Officer-in-Charge.

413. He shall ring the working-bell, and notify the buglers and drummers when to sound the calls.

414. At 4 p. m. he shall lock the doors of section-rooms, and all outside doors and windows except those on the front and rear of the building.

415. He shall see that the laundry and kitchen fires are extinguished when the laundresses and cooks leave the building.

416. He shall light up the corridors and clock-tower at the proper time, and he shall put out all lights that can be dispensed with at 10 p. m.

417. He shall have charge of the keys of the Commandant's office, clock-tower, and laundry, and of all outside doors, fire-plugs, and bath-rooms.

418. He shall keep in order the fire-lanterns in the office of the Officer-in-Charge, and in the guard-house at the upper gate.

419. The Captain of the Watch shall inspect the watchmen on duty, from time to time during the day and night, and shall see that their duties are properly performed.

420. He shall patrol the yard during the day, and occasionally at night. He shall be on duty at all entertainments in the gymnasium, and remain in attendance until the lights are extinguished.

421. He shall keep a lookout in the rear of Officers' and Cadets' quarters.

422. During the summer he shall weigh the coal, making a report to the Senior Aid ; and he shall keep an account of all anthracite coal expended during the year.

423. The Master-at-Arms shall accompany the Officer-in-Charge at f renoon inspections, and shall be responsible for the general cleanliness of all parts of the Cadets' quarters except their rooms.

424. He shall stay in the building whenever the Cadets may be absent from their quarters, and shall be responsible for property lost or stolen at such times.

425. He shall remain at his station from 6 a. m. till 10 p. m. on Saturday, and till 8 p. m. on other days, except at such times as the Commandant of Cadets may give him permission to be absent for meals and other purposes.

426. The Officer-in-Charge may give him leave for not more han one hour, for special reasons, in his discretion.

427. An assistant shall take the place of the Master-at-Arms during his absence.

XXXIX.—FORMATIONS.

428. Upon the call to any formation, Cadets shall assemble and fall in at the place designated, quietly and promptly.

429. All formations shall be of a strictly military character.

430. Formations for drills and meals shall take place, when the weather permits, on the pavement in front of the new quarters, the right of the battalion near the steps; at other times in the lower hall.

431. Prayers shall always be said inside the building.

432. Section formations shall take place in the halls of the new quarters, or on the pavement in front of the old quarters, as may be directed.

433. All cases of absence from any formation or other duty shall be reported. The reporting officer shall have no discretion in accepting excuses for absence.

434. At all formations, the order "Fall in!" shall be given three minutes after the call, and the order "Front!" one minute later. The Officer of the Day shall give the orders at section formations, and the Cadet Lieutenant-Commander at other formations.

435. During the reading of the conduct report, the divisions shall be brought to "parade rest."

436. At all formations, squad and divisional commanders shall note the dress of Cadets, and report all irregularities.

XL.—SECTION LEADERS.

437. The Cadet whose name stands first on the list of a section shall be the leader, unless otherwise ordered, and the next one shall be the second leader.

438. The section leader shall be responsible for, and report, all irregularities in dress or conduct.

439. At the given signal, the leader shall form his section, at the appointed place, in two ranks, in the order in which they stand on the list from right to left.

440. At the command, he shall call the roll of his section, and shall report all absentees to the Officer of the Day.

441. The second leader, whose station at the formation shall be two paces in rear of the centre of the section, shall assist in preserving order in his section.

442. The leader shall march his section into the section room, preserving strict military discipline and silence, the second leader taking his station as guide.

443. After the section has entered the section room, the leader shall give the order "Seats!" and report absentees to the Instructor. When dismissed by the Instructor, at the close of a recitation, the leader shall give the order "Rise!" and "March out!" He shall then form his section as before, and march to the place designated for its dismissal, where he shall break ranks.

444. Sections shall always be marched in quick time ; a section of eight, or more, in column of fours, and one of less than eight, in column of twos.

445. The section leader and second leader shall bring to all formations and recitations of their section, a list of the names in the order of the published section arrangement.

446. In the absence of the leader, the second leader shall take charge, and so on, the next on the list acting as second leader.

XLI.—SECTION-ROOMS.

447. Cadets when reciting shall stand at attention or parade rest, modified as circumstances may require.

448. They shall rise without special order when the Superintendent or the Commandant of Cadets enters the room.

449. No Cadet shall go to his quarters during the recitation of his section unless ordered to his room by the Instructor, or by some other competent officer, or unless compelled by sickness, in which case he shall report immediately to the Officer-in-Charge.

450. No Cadet shall leave the section-room without the permission of the Instructor, nor shall he ask for permission except in a case of necessity.

451. Cadets permitted to leave the section-room shall return as soon as possible, and a longer absence than ten minutes shall be reported by the Instructor to the Commandant of Cadets.

452. Cadets shall not enter section-rooms, out of recitation-hours, except on duty, or after receiving special permission.

453. No Cadet except the section leader and second leader shall bring a text-book to the formation or section-room, unless specially ordered by the Instructor. Section leaders shall be responsible for the enforcement of this rule.

XLII.—REPORT AND EXCUSES.

454. Delinquencies shall be reported by the officers responsible for the conduct of the Cadets.

455. Delinquencies at recitation, or at any other time within the knowledge of Heads of Departments or their assistants, shall be reported promptly, in writing, to the Commandant of Cadets through the Officer-in-Charge.

456. Cadet-Officers and petty officers shall forward daily to the Lieutenants of their respective divisions an abstract of all offenses occurring in their respective commands during the day. Cadet-Lieutenants shall prepare their divisional abstracts and deliver them to the Cadet-Lieutenant-Commander by 8 p. m., and he shall immediately examine and deliver them to the Officer-in-Charge.

457. Reports of irregularity, inefficiency, carelessness in the performance of duty, neglect or disobedience, shall specify in what the irregularity consisted, as laid down in the misdemeanor-book.

458. Every morning, except Sundays and holidays, the conduct-reports of the preceding day shall be published, and they shall be posted during the day.

459. Excuses shall be deposited in the boxes provided for that purpose, by 8.30 a. m. of the day following that on which the report is published.

460. No excuse shall be received after that hour unless sickness, or some other unavoidable cause which must be stated in the excuse, shall have prevented, in which case it shall be sent in without delay.

461. Form of Excuse.

Date, (of writing excuse.)

Report : A. B. absent from parade.

Excuse : I was on the sick-list, (or any other cause, as the case may be.)

Respectfully submitted.

A. B. (Signature.)

U. S. N.,
Commandant of Cadets,
U. S. Naval Academy.

462. Excuses shall be carefully written, without interlineation or blot, on a half-sheet or sheet of note-paper, as may be necessary, and shall be confined to a brief and respectful statement of facts. They shall be folded once, lengthwise, and indorsed as follows:

Excuse of

A. B. (—— class.)

Reported by

(Name of reporting-officer.)

(Date of daily conduct-report in which offense appears.)

463. All reports of absence from recitations, drills, or any other duty, or of absence from quarters at night, must be explained by a written statement, whether an excuse is offered or not.

464. Appeals for reconsideration of excuses will not be entertained after the expiration of two weeks from the date of the offense, except in cases where it was impossible to apply within that time.

XLIII.—LEAVE OF ABSENCE.

465. During the Academic year leave of absence shall not be granted by the Superintendent to any Cadet without the express sanction of the Secretary of the Navy, except in cases of urgent necessity.

466. The Superintendent may grant leave of absence to the Second Class after the June examination.

467. Applications from Cadets for leave of absence on account of ill health shall be accompanied by a certificate of the Senior Medical Officer present.

468. When a Cadet absent on leave is prevented by ill health from returning to the Academy, he must, on the first day of each month, transmit a certificate of the state of his health to the Superintendent, which shall be signed by a medical officer of the Navy when practicable, but should there be none in the vicinity a resident physician of the place must sign the same, whose standing must be attested by a magistrate or some person known to the authorities of the Academy.

469. Cadets obtaining leave of absence shall report to the Superintendent their intended place of residence, and any changes, as they may occur.

XLIV.—LIBERTY.

470. Liberty to go beyond the Academic limits shall only be granted on Saturdays and on holidays, and shall end at evening parade unless otherwise ordered; and it shall not extend beyond the immediate vicinity of Annapolis.

471. The First Class of Cadet-Midshipmen and the First Class of Cadet-Engineers, and not more than one-fourth of the three lower classes, may go on liberty at the same time; but only when deserving the privilege by good conduct.

472. A list of Cadets allowed to go on liberty shall be prepared under the direction of the Commandant of Cadets, and read out at dinner-formation on Saturday.

473. Cadets whose names have been read out at dinner-formation to go on liberty shall report themselves, on leaving the Academic limits, to the Officer of the Day, who shall be furnished with a correct list; and on returning they shall report themselves both to the Officer of the Day and to the Officer-in-Charge.

474. Cadets whose names have not been thus read out, but who have received the Superintendent's verbal permission to go on liberty, shall report to the Officer of the Day and the Officer-in-Charge, both going and returning.

475. Cadets receiving the Superintendent's written or verbal permission to go on liberty at any other time, shall report the fact, together with the limits of the time, both to the Officer-in-Charge and the Officer of the Day; and at the expiration of the time they shall report themselves to both these officers, whether they availed themselves of the permission or not, and make a statement accordingly.

476. Cadets shall not be excused from recitations or exercises or from any other duty for the purpose of seeing their friends.

XLV.—PRIVILEGES.

477. The Superintendent shall allow such amusements, from time to time, as he may think proper.

478. Cadets may be allowed to form boat-clubs and base-ball clubs, under such regulations as the Superintendent may establish.

479. The boat-flag shall be presented to the winning crew at the June regatta, and the names of the crew shall be inscribed on the staff.

480. Cadets' hops shall begin at 7.30 p. m. and end at 10 p. m., unless otherwise specially ordered upon rare occasions by the Superntendent. At the latter hour the band shall cease playing, the lights shall be turned out, and the gymasium shall be cleared.

481. Cadets shall be allowed to escort ladies to and from hops, but they shall not go beyond the Academic limits for this purpose. They shall not enter any house on returning, and shall be in their rooms before taps.

XLVI.—FIRE ORGANIZATION.

482. Cadets shall, at the fire-alarm, proceed to their stations as designated in the fire-bill.

483. The Marines shall get under arms and be posted as circumstances may require.

484. Exercise at fire-quarters shall take place at such time as the Commandant of Cadets may direct.

485. In exercising with the fire-apparatus, the Cadets shall be organized in guns' crews.

XLVII.—BARBER'S SHOP.

486. The barber's shop shall be open daily, (Sundays excepted,) from 8 a. m. till 1 p. m., and from 2 p. m. till 5 p. m., for hair-dressing, hair-cutting, shampooing, and shaving.

487. Cadets shall obtain permission of the Officer-in-Charge before visiting the barber's shop, and not more than four Cadets shall be allowed in the shop at the same time.

488. Regular days shall be assigned for each class, and members of one class shall not go to the shop on the days assigned to another class, without special permission from the Commandant of Cadets.

XLVIII.—BATHING ROOMS.

489. Cadets shall bathe at least once a week, and shall check each bath in the bath-book.

490. Cadets who take extra baths shall pay the barber six cents for each one when his towels and soap are used.

491. Loitering and disorderly conduct in the bath-rooms or basement are forbidden.

492. After bathing, the soap shall be put away and the water let off.

493. Servants in charge of the bath-rooms shall always be in readiness to attend bathers.

XLIX.—BOATS.

494. The boats of the Academy and their fittings are under the immediate control of the Commandant of Cadets, and they shall not be used without his knowledge and consent.

495. An officer shall be detailed to take charge of the boats, and he shall have sails and oars put away or secured when the boats are returned, and report their return and condition to the Commandant of Cadets.

496. Each boat shall have her recall painted on the stern-board, and the Cadet in charge shall never go out of signal distance of the flag-ship without express permission. A lookout shall be kept for the recall from the flag-ship, and when it is seen, the boat shall be brought at once to the wharf.

497. The Quartermaster in charge of the recalls shall hold himself in readiness to signal, keeping a special lookout for accidents whenever the boats are out.

498. The steam-launch shall be kept in readiness whenever Cadets may be sailing, and shall not be used for other purposes during the time they are out; in case of accident, it shall be sent out without delay.

499. The boats or their appurtenances shall not be loaned to any one not officially connected with the Academy, without the Superintendent's authority.

L.—SUPPLEMENTARY REGULATIONS.

500. All regulations necessary for the police and discipline of the Academy, not inconsistent with the foregoing, will be established by the Superintendent.

ASSISTANT TO THE COMMANDANT OF CADETS.

501. The Lieutenant Commander or Lieutenant detailed as the Assistant to the Commandant of Cadets, shall be charged with the administration of the Mess-Hall, Kitchen, and Laundry, in matters of discipline, cleanliness, and the care of the property there in use. He shall also be responsible for the efficient working of the Laundry.

502. He shall inspect the quality and the preparation of the provisions, notify the Commissary of complaints in regard to the food, and, if necessary, bring them to the notice of the Commandant of Cadets.

INDEX.

A.

Paragraph.

Absence from examination 122, 124, 125

    formation 433

    recitation, Mark to be given for 132

        Unauthorized 24

    rooms during study-hours. 312, 313

    theme-exercise 123

  Leave of. (See Leave.)

  of Commandant of Cadets 25

    Master-at-Arms. 427

    Medical Officers 66

    Officer-in-Charge 365

    Officer of the Day 410

    Section-leader 446

  Reports of 463

Absent, Offenses committed while 195

Absentees 440

Academic Board, Adjournment of 33

      Committees of 37

      Duties of 31

      how composed 28

      may establish advanced courses 109

      Meetings of, when held 30

      Presiding officer of 29

      Proceedings confidential 35

      Quorum 30

      Reports from 29

      Rules of proceedings 32

      Secretary of 34

      to determine time for examining absentees 125

    Calendar 36, 89–91, 159

    limits. 292

      Bringing articles forbidden within 169

      Fire-arms forbidden within. 189, 294

      Going beyond, without permission 169

      No disturbance within. 294

      No improper person to be brought within 190

    terms and year 89, 90

	Paragraph.
Account, Mess, Absentees to receive credit on	336
Accounts of Cadets, Monthly statement of	71
Commissary	82, 84
laborers and mechanics	72
prepared by Senior Aid	26
Storekeeper's	78
Addressing officers about marks	239
reports	240
Commandant of Cadets	235
Superintendent	231, 232
Adjutant	166
Admission	92–101
Deposit at	101
Examinations for, Committee to conduct	37
Regulations governing	31, 36, 94–98
Oath taken at	101
Traveling-expenses of candidates for	100
Advanced courses	109
final multiple of a Cadet	149
Age of candidates	94–96
Algebra	106
Alphabetically, Cadets with same average arranged	140
Analytical Geometry	106
Amusements	477
Anchor to be worn on collar	210
Annual examination, Absence from	125
Dress-parade during	115
Length of	117
papers, how marked	119
Preliminary report of	44
Programme for	37
Time	112
witnessed by Board of Visitors	116
Annual Register	36, 158, 159
Examination-papers for	47
Answering for another at roll-call	188
questions put by superior officer	196
Apparatus, Inventory of.	41
Appeals for reconsideration of excuses	464
Applications for repairs	27
for leave from Cadets	467
Officers	59
Applied Mathematics	106
Arrangement of daily conduct report	369
merit-rolls	145
rooms	301
sections	40, 104

	Paragraph.
Articles for the better government of the Navy to be read	226
supplied to Cadets from store	79
Artillery drills, Organization of	162
Assignment of section-rooms	36
Assistance, receiving unauthorized	133, 169
Associations, No Cadet to join	186
Astronomy	106
Attendants not to be sent out by Cadets	319
Audit of Commissary's accounts	82
Average, Cadets having same, how arranged	140
how computed	137
Averages, Weekly, how recorded	138

B.

Backgammon forbidden	169
Badges, Cadet-Officers'	209
Distinguished Cadets'	211
Barber's bills, how charged	68
shop	486–488
Barometer to be recorded	372, 380
Baseball-clubs	478
Bathing	489, 492
Bathing rooms, Conduct in	491
Keys of	417
Servants in	493
Baths, Extra	490
Battalion-organization, Cadet Lieutenant-Commander at	165
Beards forbidden	212
Beds, Sitting on, forbidden	306
Bell, Working	413
Bills, Cadets'	68
Board, Academic. (See Academic Board.)	
for examination of clothing	79, 80
of Visitors	116
Boat clubs	478
flag	479
house, Shell	299
Boats not to be loaned	499
Officer in charge of	495
Taking out	496
under control of Commandant of Cadets	494
Boisterous conduct forbidden	320
Books, Abstraction or mutilation of	280
for library, List of	48
kept by Commissary	84
Text, not to be brought into section-room	453
sold	193.

5

Paragraph.
Books, Text, Notice to Store-keeper about.................................. 48
    prescribed by Academic Board.............................. 31
Bowling-alley.. 221
Boxing... 106
Branches of study... 105
Breach of confinement... 183
Bugle sounds call to studies.. 223
Buglers, Inspection of.. 360
    Notice to... 413
Buildings, Charge of.. 26, 291

C.

Cadet-Lieutenants to report delinquencies 459
    Lieutenant-Commander, Duties of.............................. 165, 456
    Officers, Appointment of.. 160
        Badges of... 209
        to report delinquencies.................................. 322, 456
Cadet-organization... 160-167
    rank, Reduction of.. 175
Cadets' quarters... 301-321
    rooms, Arrangement of... 301
        Entering, during study-hours................................. 321
Calendar, Academic. (See Academic Calendar.)
Call to studies... 223
Candidates, Circulars to... 36, 97
    Examination of.. 93-99
    Expenses of... 100
    Re-examination of... 99
Cap-covers, when worn... 204
Captain of watch.. 419-422
Cards forbidden... 169
Certificate of illness.. 468
Certificates giving... 10
Chairs not to be moved back at meals till order 328
    in rooms.. 305
Change of rooms... 319
Chapel, Behavior in.. 169, 246
    Restrictions on attending evening service in..................... 249
    Service in.. 245-249
Chaplain to say prayers... 244
Chemistry... 106
Chess forbidden... 169
Children forbidden to go into public buildings....................... 297
Choir, Inspection of.. 247
Church-parties. (See Parties.)
Circulars to candidates.. 36, 97
Class-reports, Monthly..43, 86, 104

67

	Paragraph.
Class-reports, Term and year	45, 46, 86, 104
Classification of Cadets	102–104
in sections	104
Clock-tower	416, 417
Clothes, Wash	317
Clothing, Citizens', turned in	215
to be marked	206
procured by Store-keeper	74
compared with patterns	79
Clubs, Boat and base-ball	478
Coal	422
Coat, Undress, when buttoned	203
Colors of flag-staff	361
Combinations forbidden	187
Commandant of Cadets, Absence of	25
Duties of	18–24
Official intercourse with	235
Rank of	17
To command practice-ships	154
Commissary	68, 81–84
Committee in charge of library	266, 267
to conduct examination for admission	37
Communications to Navy Department	230
Unauthorized	11, 169
Written, to Superintendent	233
Company, Color	167
Drill, Organization for	162
Compensation for tuition, No person to receive	12
Competitive company-drill	114
examination for admission	93
Complaints against employés by Cadets, how made	234
as to provisions	337
made to officers	237
Conduct	168–197
at meals	332
at store	290
record, No person to have access to	22
report, daily, Arrangement of	369
copying and posting	369, 380
to be published	435, 458
submitted and entered	22
Confinement, Breach of	183
Cases of, entered in journal	372
in quarters	175
Length of	181
on board the Santee	379
Refusing to take another Cadet into	169

Paragraph.

Confinement, Restrictions under 180
   under guard 175
Conversation, Superintendent of Floor not to hold 398
   with officers about reports 240
Copying from another Cadet.. 133, 169
Correspondence, Unauthorized 11, 169
Corridors, Conduct in.............................. 320
   Lighting of 416
Course of instruction.. 105–107
   prescribed by Academic Board....................... 31
Coventry... 175, 179
Coverlets to conform to pattern 305
Curtains forbidden 303
Custody of Cadets in guard-house... 373

D.

Daily conduct-report. (See Conduct-report.)
  routine 216
Dancing.. 106
  for Fourth Class.................................... 284
  other classes...... 285
Dancing-lessons attended by Officer-in-Charge.......................... 360
Debts forbidden 185
Defacing journal.. 374
  public property 390
Defaming another Cadet.. 169
Deficiency, how determined 131
  reports..5, 6, 31, 37
Deficient Cadets, Names of, on merit-rolls 145
  not to remain at Academy................................ 31
  Recommendations as to 31
  Report to parents of 7
Delinquencies at recitation.................................. 455
  Daily report of................................ 219
  reported by Cadet-Officers 456
   Superintendents of Floors........................ 327
  reporting 454
Demerits, Limit of... 173
  number given for each offense.................................... 174
  record of misconduct 171
  Removal of.................................... 173
  Reports of................... .... 4, 5, 23
Departments... 105
Deposit of Cadets on admission................................. 101
Deprivation of leave 175
  recreation.. 175
   Length of...................................... 181

69

Paragraph.

Deprivation of recreation, Restrictions under................................. 182
Descriptive geometry 106
Designing of machinery 106
Detail for Officer of Day 362
  of daily duty 220
  of officers for practice-cruise.. 156
  of sections 53
Detailed for other than regular duty, Instructors........................... 58
Detention of sections after time 57
Directions to sections, when given.. 56
Disability, Feigning.. 169
Dismissal of Cadets from examination-room.................................. 127
  sections 56
Dismissals 169
  Secretary to inform Heads of Departments of.......................... 88
  to be entered in journal.. 372
  to be read out at parade.. 355
Disobedience... 169
Dispensary, Hours for visiting... 236
  Regulations of 65
Disqualifications of Cadets, Physical or mental............................. 64
Distinguished Cadets, Badges of 150, 211
Disturbances forbidden... 294
Divine service 244-252
Divisions, artillery exercise.. 162
  great-gun exercise... 161
  infantry drill.. 162
Doors to be locked 414
Drawing 106
Dress, Full 198, 201
  No part of one, to be worn with another 207
  parade during annual examination...................................... 115
  Uniform for... 201
  When held... 225
  Working... 200, 202
Dressing-gowns 214
Drill, Competitive company 114
  Extra 175
  Knives worn at seamanship.. 213
  not attended by Cadets under confinement 180
  Officer of Day.. 366
  Suspension of 91, 120, 229
  When to take place.. 224
Drills, Charge of.. 19
  to be entered in journal.. 372
Drummer notified to sound calls 413

70

		Paragraph.
Duties, Extra		175
Duty not to be performed by Cadets under suspension		179
Dynamics		106

E.

Elective courses		109
Marks in		142
Elementary branches, Cadets subject to examination in, at all times		129
Embarkation of Cadets for practice-cruise		153
Employés in hospital		265
Engineers, Cadet, Corps-badge of		210
Practice-cruise		155
English studies		106
Entering Cadets' rooms during study-hours		321
unoccupied rooms, forbidden		319
Entertainments, Cadets under suspension not allowed at		179
Dress to be worn at		201
in rooms forbidden		191
Entrance, Main, to be used by Cadets		314
Examination for admission		92–99
Committee to conduct		37
Regulations prepared for		31, 36
papers, language and spelling to be marked		141
two Instructors to mark		119
physical, for passing to higher grades		128
of candidates		98
questions, for Register		47
rooms, Dismissal of Cadets from		127
Leaving before completion of work		126
Examinations		110–129
Absence from		122, 124, 125
Annual. (See Annual Examinations.)		
in elementary branches held at any time		129
Length of		117
Monthly. (See Monthly Examinations.)		
on completed work		111
uncompleted work		111, 113
regulated by Academic Board		31
Semi-annual. (See Semi-annual Examinations.)		
Semi-monthly. (See Semi-monthly Examinations.)		
to be entered in journal		372
written and oral, Directions about		118
Exchanging books or articles		193
Excuse, Cadets allowed to make		178
Excused Cadets to report at sick-call		257
from recitation, Cadets		258
to see friends, No Cadets		476

Paragraph.

Excused list... 62, 255
   What Cadets are... 254-256
Excuses, Acceptance of 433
   and reports, when prepared... 370
   Form of... 461, 462
   Reconsideration of.. 464
   Time and place of handing in.. 459, 460
Exercise in gymnasium.. 283
   Organization for great-gun... 161
         Infantry and Artillery 162
         Naval Tactics 164
         Seamanship....................................... 163
Exercises, Academic, suspended at examinations 120
         on holidays 91
         other times......................... 229
Expenses of candidates.. 100
Explanation of absence.. 463
Extra drills. (See Drills.)
Extra meals. (See Meals.)

F.

Fabrication of machinery.. 106
Families of Officers to observe regulations 296
Feigning illness or disability... 63, 169
Fencing 106
Final average, how computed 137
Fire alarm 482
   department, Charge of.. 18
   Inspection to guard against.. 351
   lanterns 418
   organization 18, 435
   plugs, Keys of 417
   quarters, Exercise at 484, 485
Fire-arms and fire-works not to be discharged 189, 294
Fires, Laundry and kitchen, extinguished 415
First Class.. 103
   term, examinations 111
      Extent of... 89, 90
   year's course 107
Flag, Boat... 479
   Prize-company.. 114, 167
Flag-ship, guide in hoisting colors...................................... 361
   Lookout from 496
Flag-staff, Colors of. (See Colors.)
Foils, Breaking 286
Food and furniture not to be brought into mess-hall...................... 334
        taken from mess-hall...................... 333

Paragraph.

Form of excuse. (See Excuse.)

Formations 428, 436
  general, Cadet Lieutenant-Commander at 165
  Position of Adjutant at 166
  Conduct at.. 436
  for drills and meals 430
  Keeping order at 396
  Military character of 429
  No text-books at 453
  Officer-in-Charge at 346
   of the Day at.. 366
  Orders at... 434
  Orders read at... 356
  Section-leader at 439, 440
  Superintendent of Floor at....................................... 396
Fourth Class.. 103
French 106
Furniture and food in mess-hall. (See Food.)
Furniture, Responsibility for, in rooms 404

G.

Games of chance forbidden 169
Gas in rooms, Burning 308
   after taps 352
Gate, upper, Cadets to use 300
General passes not to be given... 293
Geometry 106
Gestures, Using reproachful.. 169
Government of Naval Academy 1-16
Graduating merit-roll 6, 146
  multiple.. 146
Graduation, Physical examination prior to............................... 123
Great-gun exercise. Organization. (See Exercise.)
   Practical instruction in 106
Grounds.. 291-300
  Charge of 26, 291
Guard, Confinement under. (See Confinement.)
  duty 175
  house not to be visited 238
   Responsibility of Cadets in 378
Gunnery 106
  Duties of Head of Department of................................... 50
Gunpowder forbidden... 189
Gymnasium 281-286
  Dancing-exercise at. (See Dancing.)
  hours to be used... 281, 283
  Officer-in-Charge at.. 360

73

	Paragraph.
Gymnasium parties	380
Restrictions of Fourth Class at	284
Gymnastics	106

H.

Hair cut short	212
cutting	486
Hands not to be carried in pockets	203
Hazing	170
Heads of Departments, duties	39–50
present at oral examinations	118
to make detail of sections	53
History	106
Holiday	91
Hops	480, 481
Officer-in-Charge at	360
Hospital	253–265
Attendants at	262, 265
Patients in	262, 264
Regulations of	65
Visiting	263
Hotels, Not to visit	184
Hours of recitation posted in rooms	309
study. (See Study-hours.)	
Hygiene, Maintenance of	61

I.

Illness at other times than regular sick-call	250
Feigning	169
Inattention of servants. (See Servants.)	
Indulgences, Cadets under suspension not to apply for	179
Infantry drill	162
tactics	106
Injury to public property	293
Inspection, Battalion	347
Choir	247
Floor	380, 385, 387, 388
Mess-hall	323, 324
of provisions	325
rooms	391–393
servants	323
Sunday	226, 311
Instruction, by whom given	40, 51
Course of	105–107
Instructors, Applications of, for leave of absence	59
as Officer-in-Charge	338
Dismissal of Cadets from examination-room by	127

Paragraph

Instructors, Dismissal of Cadets from section-room by......................... 56
    Duties of.. 51-60
    not to hold communication with Cadets about marks........... 60
    to note daily marks.. 52
    ordered to extra duty.. 58
    responsible for order of sections 54
    to inform Cadets when zero is given 134
    to hear sections in rotation................................... 53
    to mark examination-papers 119
Instruments, Musical, when forbidden... 310
Insulting watchmen... 169
Intercourse, Official. (See Official Intercourse.)
Intermission, Marks not given during 136
Intoxication 169
Invalids in hospital 65
Issue of articles to Cadets... 76

J.

Jack-knives, when to be worn.. 213
Journal, Contents of.. 372
    Defacing... 374
    signed by Officer-in-Charge.................................... 358
    taken to Superintendent.. 380

K.

Keys, Charge of 417

L.

Lamps in yard.. 409
Languages, Modern 106
Launch, Steam.. 498
Laundress's bills 68
Law.. 106
Leave, Deprivation of.. 175
Leave of absence, Application for 59, 467
    Residence during... 469
    Return from.. 15
    Sickness during.. 468
    to Cadets not granted during session 465
Leave of absence to Officers 14
    to Second Class.. 466
Leaving examination-rooms 126
    mess-hall 329
    section-rooms.. 451
Length of course... 107
    examinations 117
    service required... 101

Paragraph.

Liberty at irregular times 475
    book, names in.. 371
    going on and returning from............................... 473
    Limitations of 470, 471
    list 380, 472
    Verbal permission to go on 474, 475
    when granted... 470
Librarian, Duties of 268, 270
Library............. 266-280
    List of books wanted in................................... 48
Lieutenant-Commander, Cadet. Reports........................ 456
Lieutenants, Cadet. Reports 456
Lights in rooms..............................308, 352, 380, 385, 405, 416
Limits. (See Academic limits.)
Liquors forbidden 169
Lookout for boats.. 496, 497

M.

Mail, by whom distributed.................................... 400
Main entrance. (See Entrance.)
Marine engines 106
Marines 18
    at fire-alarm 483
Mark, Elective course....................................... 142
    of zero. (See Zero.)
Marked, Clothing to be....................................... 206
Marks.. 130-142
    Communication with Instructors about..................... 60, 239
    given before first Monday................................ 135
    not given during intermission 136
    noted by Instructors..................................... 52
    Scale of... 130
    Weekly, for one recitation............................... 139
Master-at-Arms, Duties of.................................... 423-427
Meals, Dress at.. 330
    Extra 335
    Officer-in-Charge at..................................... 322
    served in rooms 335
    Time allowed for... 327
Mechanical drawing 106
Mechanics, branch of study 106
    Payment of... 72
Medical Board 64
    Officer............. 253-263
    Senior. (See Senior Medical Officer.)
    Officers all not to be absent............................ 66
    stores, Charge of.. 61

	Paragraph.
Mental examination of candidates	98
Merit-rolls	143–150
Arrangement of	144, 145
Class-reports used in preparing	46
Contents of, for Navy Department	147
Grading	146
when and by whom made out	6, 38, 143
Mess-account, Absentees who have credit on	336
arrangements on practice-cruise	154
hall	322–337
Inspection of	323, 324
Leaving	329
Persons not to be brought into	190
table, Conduct at	331
Messenger of Superintendent or Commandant of Cadets	242
Midshipman, Cadet, Badge of	210
Misbehavior, Attention of Cadets called to	197
Misconduct, Demerits a record of	171
Watchmen to report	412
Misdemeanor-book	174
to be used in reporting	457
Missiles not to be thrown	294
Modern languages	106
Molesting Cadets of Fourth Class	170
Money, Payment of, to Cadets	69
Monthly averages, how computed	137
class-reports	43
examinations, Absence from	124
Length of	117
Programme of	49
to be written	118
Mortar-practice	106
Moustaches forbidden	212
Multiple, Final, of Cadets advanced	149
turned back	148
Graduating	146
Multiples, how determined	144
Musical instruments, when forbidden	319
Mutilation of books, Wilful	280

N.

Nails not to be driven in rooms	303
Naval architecture	106
tactics	106
organization for drill	164
Navigation	106

	Paragraph.
Navy Department, Communications to	230
regulations to be observed	168
Night-quarters	227
Notices not to be posted in grounds	293

O.

Oak-leaves on collar, Cadet-Engineers	210
Oath taken at admission	101
Obey, Failing to	160
Obscene language	169
Offenses reported by Superintendent of Floor	389
Offenses to be reported to Superintendent	177
Office of Commandant of Cadets not to be visited	238
Officer-in-Charge	238
Superintendent	232
Officer-in-Charge	338–361
Absence of	365
Officers to act as	338, 339
old quarters, Duties of	360, 361
pass all orders	359
Uniform of	342
Officer of the Day	362–380
relieved at examinations and lectures	121
Officers, application for leave	59
assigned to duty at Naval Academy	8
Cadet	160
Badges of	209
reporting delinquencies	456
detailed for practice-cruise	156
quarters, Hours for visiting	236
Official intercourse	230–243
with Commandant of Cadets	235
Superintendent	231, 232
Official records kept by Secretary	86
Oral examinations	118
Order, Preservation of	380, 392
Orders at formations	330
meals	327
parade	356
when official	241
Ordnance and gunnery. (See Gunnery.)	
Instructions	106
Organization, Cadet	160–167
Outfit at graduation	70
of Cadets at admission	101
Overcoats and overshoes, when to be worn	204

78

P.

Paragraph.

Papers, Examination. (See Examination.)

Parents, Notices to.. 4, 7

Parties, Church 250, 251

Pass-books... 289

Passes, by whom issued 375

    No general... 298

Patients in hospital..65, 262, 264

Patterns, Articles to conform to..,............................. 206

Periods 216, 221

Periodicals taken by Cadets 192

    taken from library... 277

Permission to go on liberty, Verbal 474, 475

Physical examination. (See Examinations.)

Physics.. 106

Pictures not allowed 304

Pistol-gallery 281

Playing on musical instruments................................. 319

Pockets, Hands not in 208

Police 18, 21

Postage-account of Cadets.................................... 68

Practical exercises 106

Practice-cruise... 151–157

Prayers.. 244, 431

Preliminary reports of semi-annual and annual examinations 44

Preparation of merit-rolls....................................38, 46, 143–150

Presents, No person to receive 12

Prevarication 169

Prize-flag 167

Profane language 169

Proficiency, Minimum of....................................... 131

Programmes of monthly examinations......................... 49

    semi-annual and annual examinations 37

    semi-annual and annual examinations, when published......... 110, 112

Property stolen in absence of Cadets........................... 424

Provisions, Inspection of.................................... 325

Provoking language... 169

Public correspondence, Secretary to file.................... 87

    entertainments, No Cadet to attend..................... 184

    property, Injury to... 280, 293

        Preservation of 395

        Responsibility for......................................26, 41, 405

Publications, causing, All persons 11

    Cadets 169

Punishmen, Demerits not a................................... 171

    for offenses committed on leave 195

Paragraph.

Punishment, No, inflicted without Superintendent's order 177
         Studies not to be discontinued by Cadets under 180
Punishment 175

Q.

Quarters, at night 227
     Cadets 301–321
         cleanliness of, Master-at-Arms responsible for parts of 423
     Confinement to 175
     Going to, during recitation 449
     No person to be brought into 190
     Repairs of Officers' 27
Questions, Examination, for Register 47

R.

Rain-coats 204
Rank, Reduction of Cadet 175
Recitation, Periods of 221
Recitations, Daily, arranged by Academic Board 108
     Delinquencies at 455
     not to be attended by Cadets under confinement. 180
     Officer of Day not to attend 366
     Superintendent of Floor not to attend 397
     Suspension of 120, 229
Reconsideration of excuses 464
Record of conduct, No person to have access to 22
     offenses and demerits 172
     punishments 172
Recreation, Deprivation of. 175, 161
Re-examination of candidates prohibited 99
Refusing to take another Cadet into confinement 169
Regatta, June 479
Register. (See Annual Register.)
Regulations, examination for admission 31, 92–101
     Hospital 65
     Navy, to be observed 168
     Persons subject to 9
     for quarters, posted in rooms 309
     Supplementary 500
     Violations of 13, 21
Re-instatements, Secretary to inform Heads of Departments of 88
Relative-standing reports 4, 6, 31
     weight of branches 31
     marks 31
Release of Cadets from confinement, put in Journal 372
Relief, Officer of Day to conduct 380
Relieving Officer of Day and Superintendents of Floors for examination 121

	Paragraph.
Religious services	244, 252
Removal from service, only by Secretary of Navy	176
of demerits	173
Repairs of buildings	20, 26, 27
Reporting return from leave	15
Report, Daily conduct, posted	458
submitted and entered	22
misconduct, All Officers to	13, 21
Reports. (See Table.)	
Academic Board	29, 31
Reports, Addressing officers about	240
by whom made	454
Class, separate for Cadet-Midshipmen and Cadet-Engineers	104
of delinquencies	55, 219
of demerits	23
Instructors', to be filed	357
Monthly class	43
must be specific	457
of absence must be explained	463
of persons unfitted for duty by illness	62
Preliminary, semi-annual, and annual examinations	44
Scandalous or unusual	353
of semi-monthly examinations	43
of Term and year	45, 46
to be investigated	178
to Navy Department, made out by Secretary	87
of unsatisfactory recitations	42
separate, for Cadet-Midshipmen and Cadet-Engineers	104
Reprimand, Public	175
Reproachful language	169
Requests made of Officers	237
requiring immediate attention	370
Requisitions, Cadets'	287, 288
of Heads of Departments, Yearly	48
Reserved pay	70
Residence of Cadets on leave	469
Resignations, Secretary to inform Heads of Departments of	88
Resignations to be entered in journal	372
read at parade	355
Responsibility, relieved from by reporting offender	196
Restaurant, No Cadets to visit	184
Restrictions of Fourth Class at gymnasium	282
on Cadets on sick or excused list	260
Reveille, Duties of Cadets at	218
Rhetoric	106
Roll-call, Answering for another Cadet	188

                                                                Paragraph.
Roll-call at formations   440
         morning, Inspection at...   380
Rolls of the Academy   86
Room, Entertainment and cooking forbidden in   191
         responsibility in... 404, 406
Rooms, Cadets' 301–321
                   Arrangement of   301
                   Dressing-gowns in...   214
                   Inspection of.   (See Inspection.)
                   Meals in   335
                   Unauthorized articles in   362
                   when visited by Officer of the Day   376
         Cadets to go to..   384
         Unoccupied 319, 394
Routine, Changes in...   217
         Daily..   216
         duty of Officer of the Day   380
Rugs, conform to pattern   305

                              S.

Salutations, Exchange of, in rooms 310, 349
Salutes...   243
Scale of marks..   130
Seamanship...   106
         drill, Organization for...   163
         Head of Department of, to assist Commandant of Cadets.........   50
Seats at meals not to be changed...   326
Second Class   103
         leader   441
         term, extent of..   89, 90
         year's course..   107
Secretary, Duties of   85–88
         Visiting office of...   236
         of Academic Board   34
         of the Navy, charge of Naval Academy...........................   1
                   Removal of Cadets ordered only by.   176
Section-arrangements..   104
                   sent to Commandant of Cadets   40
Section, Detention of, after time......   57
Section-formations, where held   432
Section-leaders... 437–446
         may bring text-books.....................................   453
Section-rooms 447–453
                   Assignment of   36
                   Discipline of..54, 443, 455
                   Heads of Departments shall visit   40
                   Leaving 449, 450

	Paragraph.
Sell any articles, Cadets not to	193
Semi-annual examinations, Absence from	125
Duration of	117
papers, how marked	119
Preliminary report of	44
Programme of	37
Time of	110
Semi-monthly examinations, Absence from	124
Duration of	117
Reports of	43
to be written	118
Senior Aid	26, 27
Medical Officer. Duties of	61–66
to conduct physical examinations	128
Serious offenses	169
Servants at mess-hall, Inspection of	323
Inattention of	337
not to be sent out by Cadets	319
enter public buildings	297
to obey regulations	296
Service, Religious	244–252
Shell-boat house	299
Ship-building	106
Shoes to be blacked, where put	318
Sick Cadets	257
Sick-call	259
Sick-list	253, 254
Names removed from	258
sent to Commandant of Cadets	62
Sick-lists filed	357
Sickness at other times than sick-call	259
during leave	468
Signals, Exercise in	106
to be sounded	367
Sitting at windows	306
up after taps	352
Smoking forbidden	169, 295
Solitary confinement	175
Spanish	106
Specimen questions for Register	47
Standing, Relative	4–6, 31
Star, Cadets designated by	150, 211
Statements, Making unauthorized	10
Statics	106
Stationery, Requisitions for	48
Steam-Engineering	106

Paragraph.

Steam-launch to be kept in readiness 498
Stones not to be thrown 294
Store 287-290
    Articles authorized in 75
    Hours for visiting 236
Store-keeper 74-78
    bills, how charged 68
    notice of text-books needed 48
    time when required to be at store 77
Studies suspended 91, 120, 229
Study, Branches of 103
    hours, Absence from room during 312, 313
        Duration of 222
        Visiting during 312
    Periods of 221
Sunday, Inspection of rooms 311
    parade 226
    Observance of 169, 252
Superintendent 2-7
    Addressing the 231
    All offenses reported to 177
    All punishments ordered by 177
Superintendent of Floor or Building 381-401
        Reports of 380
        to be relieved for examinations 121
        to report absence from rooms 313
    rooms 402-408
Supplementary regulations 500
Supplies, Bills for 73
Surveying 106
Suspension 175, 179
    Cases of, entered in journal 372
    of studies 91, 120, 229
Sweeping rooms 406
Swimming 106

T.

Table-cloths, conform to pattern 305
Tactical instruction in charge of Commandant of Cadets 19
Tactics, Infantry and Naval 106
Talking loud in rooms or corridors 320
Taps, Inspection at 365
    Lights after 352
Target-practice 106
    entered in journal 372
Temperature of rooms 350
Term class-reports 45

84

Paragraph.

Text-books not to be brought to formation 453
    not to be sold 193
    Notice to store-keeper of 48
    prescribed by Academic Board 31
Themes, Exercises in 106
    to be made up 123
    Unauthorized assistance in preparing 133, 169
Thermometer to be recorded 372, 380
Third Class 103
    year's course 107
Throwing from windows 306
    missiles 294
Time-form to be posted 309
Tobacco forbidden 169
Traducing another Cadet 169
Transoms 307
Treasurer 67-73
Treasurer's Office, Hours for visiting 236
Tuition, No compensation for ...., ... 12
Turned back, Multiple of Cadets 148

U.

Unauthorized articles not allowed in rooms 302
    assistance 133, 169
Uniform of Cadets 198-215
    Officer-in-Charge 342
    Officer of Day 363
    Superintendents of Floors 382
Unsatisfactory recitations, Reports of 42, 104

V.

Verbal permission to go on liberty 474, 475
Vessels for practice-cruise 151
Violations of regulations to be reported 13, 21
Visit Officers' quarters, No Cadet under suspension to 179
Visiting during study-hours 312, 316
    on other floors 399
Visitors, Board of 116
    to be received by Officer of the Day 364
Visits of high officials entered in journal 372

W.

Warning-roll 228, 380
    to deficient Cadets 5
Washing, Clothes for 317
    of room 316

                                                                    Paragraph.
Watch, Captain of. (See Captain.)
    Extra 175
Watches, seamanship drill.. 163
Watchmen.. 18, 409–422
    Insulting or offering violence to................................ 169
    under orders of Officer of the Day.............................. 368, 411
Water-closets, Route to 315
Weekly averages, how recorded.. 138
    marks for single recitation, how computed........................ 139
    reports, Instructors'.. 52, 104
Weight, Relative, of marks.. 31
Whiskers forbidden 212
White caps and trowsers, when worn 205
Windows, Sitting at... 306
    Throwing from. 306
Wine forbidden 169
Working-dress... 200, 202
Workmen, Control of 26
Written exercises, marking.. 141
    to be made up 123

                                Y.
Yearly class-reports.. 45, 46

                                Z.
Zero given as a mark 130, 132–134

www.ingramcontent.com/pod-product-compliance
Lightning Source LLC
Chambersburg PA
CBHW021416090426
42742CB00009B/1166